STUDIES IN ENGLISH LITERATURE No. 57

General Editor

David Daiches

Professor of English, The School of English
and American Studies, The University of Sussex

SHAKESPEARE:

MEASURE FOR MEASURE

by

NIGEL ALEXANDER

Professor of English,
University of London, Queen Mary College

EDWARD ARNOLD

© NIGEL ALEXANDER, 1975

First published 1975
by Edward Arnold (Publishers) Ltd,
25 Hill Street, London W1X 8LL

Cloth edition ISBN: 0 7131 5809 3
Paper edition ISBN: 0 7131 5810 7

All Rights Reserved. No part of this publication may be reproduced, stored in a retrieval system, or transmitted, in any form or by any means, electronic, mechanical, photocopying, recording or otherwise, without the prior permission of Edward Arnold (Publishers) Ltd.

This book is published in two editions. The paperback edition is sold subject to the condition that it shall not, by way of trade or otherwise, be lent, resold, hired out, or otherwise circulated without the publisher's prior consent in any form of binding or cover other than that in which it is published and without a similar condition including this condition being imposed on the subsequent purchaser.

Printed in Great Britain by
The Camelot Press Ltd, Southampton

General Preface

The object of this series is to provide studies of individual novels, plays and groups of poems and essays which are known to be widely read by students. The emphasis is on clarification and evaluation; biographical and historical facts, while they may be discussed when they throw light on particular elements in a writer's work, are generally subordinated to critical discussion. What kind of work is this? What exactly goes on here? How good is this work, and why? These are the questions that each writer will try to answer.

It should be emphasized that these studies are written on the assumption that the reader has already read carefully the work discussed. The objective is not to enable students to deliver opinions about works they have not read, nor is it to provide ready-made ideas to be applied to works that have been read. In one sense all critical interpretation can be regarded as foisting opinions on readers, but to accept this is to deny the advantages of any sort of critical discussion directed at students or indeed at anybody else. The aim of these studies is to provide what Coleridge called in another context 'aids to reflection' about the works discussed. The interpretations are offered as suggestive rather than as definitive, in the hope of stimulating the reader into developing further his own insights. This is after all the function of all critical discourse among sensible people.

DAVID DAICHES

Contents

Preface

All quotations from Shakespeare are from the *Complete Works* edited by Peter Alexander, London 1951. Quotations from the *Basilicon Doron* of King James VI and I are from the edition by J. Craigie for the Scottish Text Society, Edinburgh 1944.

I am grateful to Rosalind Miles and the University of Birmingham for permission to examine unpublished dissertations and to Dr Stanley Wells for all his help and patience. Peter Alexander's trustees permitted me to consult unpublished papers.

Among the many intellectual debts incurred in the writing of this book I am conscious of particularly heavy ones to Ernest Schanzer and David Lloyd Stevenson, to Alastair Fowler and Frances Yates, and to Herbert S. Weil, Jr who generously gave me the full measure of his own work on the play. I hope that they, and all others, will not be too offended by the partial use I have made of their work in the attempt to pattern out this judgement.

I should like to thank the staff of the British Library and the University of Nottingham Library for their help.

NIGEL ALEXANDER

A bawd, sir? Fie upon him! He will discredit our mystery.

1 Comedy or Problem Play?

Measure for Measure is a comedy of accurate design and subtle psychological balance. The care with which it has been constructed ensures a smooth and swift-running theatrical performance. The jokes have been well pointed and prepared, requiring only moderate competence to make them work on the stage. The cunning of the characterization has caused generations of actors, readers, spectators and commentators to pause and ask if more is meant than meets the eye and ear. It is a play which appears to provoke the audience to question the necessity or probability of the conduct represented on stage—and such questions lead up and down through the most tangled thickets of political or moral philosophy. This makes formidable demands upon the actors. It is not difficult for them to grasp the play's basic design and convey the story to an audience. Character is counterpoised with character and act weighed against act with a precision that is, in some cases, exactly mathematical. Their problem is that this finely adjusted theatrical instrument does not produce the mechanical moral promised by the play's title. In terms of plot, character or the operation of the judging mind, measure signally fails to answer to measure.

One answer to this problem is to assert that it does not exist. On this view the play is a perfectly normal comedy and any discrepancy or discord is simply produced by a critical imagination failing to adapt to the most ordinary conventions of the stage. This belief that the problem is only in the eye of the confused beholder has the attraction of simplicity but is not borne out by the stage history of the play or the consensus of commentary. In an illuminating thesis Rosalind Miles has pointed out that actors and critics appear to find difficulty with the play from an early stage and that those difficulties remain fairly constant and predictable throughout its history.[1] There is, however, a more serious objection to this view than the large number of opposed voices. It implies that there is not much difference between *Measure for Measure* and *As You Like It* or

[1] Rosalind Miles, *The Criticism of 'Measure for Measure'* (M.A. Thesis University of Birmingham 1966) and *A Study of 'Measure for Measure'* (Ph.D. Thesis University of Birmingham 1968).

Twelfth Night. I believe that it can be demonstrated, in plain and evident dramatic terms, that *Measure for Measure* is a very different kind of comedy and that this is, in itself, one of the most significant facts about the play. This alteration in Shakespeare's treatment of comic convention, and the questions this seems to have inspired, make it reasonable to call *Measure for Measure* a difficult play.

This difficulty may be the result of accident or design. One can argue that there is every indication that the play was intended to fulfil the promise of its title and that an audience in 1604 might be expected to accept the play at exactly its face value. The failure of later ages to follow their example may be due to obscurities or inconsistencies in the original story, to some notable failure of execution on the part of the dramatist, or it may have been something that happened gradually as changing fashions in manners and morals rendered obsolete the basic assumptions on which the plot is founded. For whatever reason, the play must now, following this argument, be accounted a failure. Those who believe, as I do, that the play was deliberately contrived by Shakespeare to contradict the obvious platitude and illuminate other meanings of *Measure for Measure* are committed to some version of the view that this is a problem play. The term 'problem play' seems to have been first applied to it by F. S. Boas in *Shakespeare and his Pedecessors* (1896) and passed into general critical currency with W. W. Lawrence's *Shakespeare's Problem Comedies* (1931). Since 1875, when Edward Dowden first grouped *Troilus and Cressida*, *All's Well That Ends Well* and *Measure for Measure* together and described the last as 'dark', the play has been endlessly classified and reclassified.

2 The Text

The most appropriate way of beginning the examination of these problems is to consider the nature of the text of the play. It has survived only in one version—that prepared by Shakespeare's fellow actors, John Heminges and Henry Condell, for the collected edition of the plays published in 1623 and now generally known as the First Folio. It is generally agreed that it belongs to a group of plays which were copied out by Ralph Crane, a professional scrivener, before they were delivered to the printers. He may have prepared this copy from Shakespeare's own papers, from the theatrical prompt book, or from some other source. Certain features in the text have caused some editors, notably John Dover Wilson in his New Cambridge edition of 1922, to suggest that the text is corrupt and contains material by some other dramatist. These arguments have been admirably surveyed and, in general, rejected by J. W. Lever in the New Arden edition.

The matter, however, is worth further consideration since the very features which suggested corruption to earlier editors can be cited as evidence that the surviving text represents Shakespeare's original intentions very closely and prove that it is a play of a very special kind. These features are, in brief:

1   The presence of certain characters, such as the Justice and Julia, who seem important to the play yet have very few lines.
2   The nature of Lucio and his conversation with the gentlemen. The fact that Mistress Overdone in I.ii could be thought to be expressing surprise at the news of the proclamation when she has already declared herself an eyewitness of Claudio's arrest.
3   The strange quality and content of the Duke's two rhyming soliloquies.
4   Possible confusion over the time scheme in IV. iii.

It is, of course, easy for mistakes to creep in during the process of transferring the play to a fair copy and then, through the work of the compositors, to a printed text. But, equally, it is remarkable that these anomalies are all closely connected with the major literary and dramatic puzzles of the play—puzzles which are created by the nature of the Duke, his relationship to Lucio and the bawds, and his control, or lack of it, over the conduct of Angelo and Isabella.

One feature of Crane's work which has tended to obscure the relationship between the textual and literary problems is his habit of dividing the plays up into acts and scenes. This later fashion was not Shakespeare's own working practice. It seems evident that his unit of composition was the scene, not the act, and that a scene came to an end once the stage was cleared of all the actors on it.[2] If we take this as a principle, and compare it with Crane's division reproduced in the Folio, the following pattern emerges:

Table: The first column shows Crane's divisions by act and scene. The second column indicates 'clear stage' scene divisions.

I.i	1	The Duke delivers their commission to Angelo and Escalus.
I.ii		Lucio and two gentlemen, Mistress Overdone and Pompey.
I.iii	2	Claudio and Lucio. Lucio has not left the stage. Lever and many other editors treat this as part of scene two.
I.iv	3	The Duke and Friar Thomas.
I.v.	4	Isabella and Lucio with the news of Claudio's sentence.
II.i	5	The examination of Froth and Pompey by Angelo and Escalus.
II.ii	6	Isabella's first interview with Angelo.
II.iii	7	The Duke disguised and the Provost.
II.iv	8	Angelo's second interview with Isabella. He offers measure for measure, chastity against Claudio's life.
III.i	9	The prison scene between Isabella and Claudio. The Duke disguised assumes control and proposes another measure for measure: substitution of Mariana for Isabella.
IV.i	10	Mariana at the moated grange.
IV.ii	11	The prison on the night of Mariana's substitution. The order for Claudio's execution arrives. The Duke disguised proposes a new measure for measure—the substitution of Barnadine for Claudio.
IV.iii	12	Barnadine refuses execution. Substitution of Ragizone's head introduces another measure for measure.

[2] M. Rose, *Shakespearean Design* (Cambridge, Mass. 1972) and E. Jones, *Scenic Form in Shakespeare* (Oxford 1971).

The play falls into sixteen scenes and divides exacly into eight and eight. The first sequence comes to an end when Angelo proposes his infamous bargain to Isabella. The next eight scenes are concerned with the way in which the Duke frustrates Angelo and re-establishes justice in Vienna. The Duke's assumption of control of the action is precisely marked in scenes ix and x by the rhyming soliloquies which have caused so much trouble. It can now be seen that they are in this admittedly strange form because Shakespeare wished his audience to take special note of the change that had taken place in the action. The first of these changes is the Duke's assumption of an active role. The second is the introduction of Mariana, the girl who restores grace to the play because she is able to comply with Angelo's request in charity and chastity since the act makes her his wife. She appears, that is, to yield to Angelo's demand for fornication—a demand whose supply is the normal function of Mistress Overdone—and in so yielding releases him from that sin into the freedom of marriage. There is, however, another sin that can yet be laid to Angelo's charge. Despite the apparent satisfaction of his lust he still intends to murder Claudio—and from that sin he is only redeemed by the prayers of Mariana, of Isabella, and the Duke's preservation of Claudio. The movement of the play is, therefore, Angelo's plot, the Duke's countermeasures and then the further effort which is necessary when Angelo persists in his murderous course.

Almost every commentator has pointed out this progression from false justice to true, and from merciless rigour to merciful grace. In the action of the play false justice is met by true after scene viii, but after scene x only grace and mercy can save Angelo from the full rigour of the law. At the time that Shakespeare created *Measure for Measure* eight was a number regularly associated with justice.[3] Furthermore in *Basilicon Doron* King

---

[3] Macrobius, *Commentary on the Dream of Scipio*. Tr. and ed. W. H. Stahl (New York 1952), 'The Pythagoreans, indeed, called the number eight justice' (p. 98). It is a number which might have appealed to Shakespeare since Jonson considered eight squares with sixteen masquers appropriate to his throne of beauty. (See p. 23.)

James himself expresses, as one of the commonplaces of theology, the idea that the number ten is, through the Ten Commandments, the number associated with the law and justice of the Old Testament while six, being the sum of the four Gospels taken with the Acts and Epistles of the Apostles, embodies the grace of the New Testament which fulfilled and superseded the law.[4] If this is not coincidental, it implies that Shakespeare has built a play called *Measure for Measure* in a form which reflects with a certain mathematical precision its central concepts of justice, grace and mercy. There are grounds for believing that this was indeed his intention.   The argument now depends upon the literary and historical analysis of the play rather than textual or bibliographical details. It must be followed therefore as it is presented in the course of this study but its conclusions may, for convenience, briefly be summarized here.

1   The play was written to interest King James VI and I and may have been specifically designed for his first Christmas at Whitehall.

2   It contains compliments to the court and also includes recognizable features of James's own political philosophy as set out in *Basilicon Doron*.

3   It also makes use of a stock of imagery which was traditional at court festivals throughout Europe. One aspect of the masques and triumphs presented at court was the return of the just virgin Astraea to inaugurate reforms leading to a new golden age.[5] Shakespeare changed his sources to insist upon Isabella's virginity, thus associating her with Astraea. The presentation of a play about a just virgin and her union with a prudent and merciful ruler is entirely in keeping with the other shows and triumphs designed to welcome James to his new country and capital.

4   The play is therefore concerned with important political and religious questions of justice, grace and mercy which could only be presented upon the stage in the form of a comedy about a fictional state.

5   Yet it should not be treated simply as a courtly compliment since Shakespeare deliberately changed his comic method in order to emphasize the difficulties of this union of mercy and justice.

The Duke may share some of the king's opinions but he is hardly a portrait of King James. He may be a controlling and reassuring figure of comedy who suggests that all will be well. The chosen method, however, inevitably brings him into contact with the bawds and inhabitants of the

[4] *Basilicon Doron*, pp. 33–5.
[5] Frances A. Yates, *Astraea* (London 1975).

stews and forces him to face the fact that there are aspects of human nature which cannot be controlled by the methods which first prompted him to make Angelo his deputy. The play suggests that true government is neither puritanical nor permissive but strong enough and generous enough to unite even Angelo or Lucio, even the Duke and Isabella, in harmony and concord where measure answers to measure. It ought to have made its royal spectator reflect on whether he was capable of such government. There is no evidence that he was troubled by such thoughts but the play has remained to cause generations of spectators to ask whether this desirable process which fuses mercy and justice is practical or possible.

This interpretation provides an explanation of many of the puzzling features of the play. Doubts about the formal structure of the play are shown to be due to a failure to appreciate the convention of courtly compliment which Shakespeare used for his design. Questions about the play's moral structure are caused by Shakespeare's refusal simply to follow a customary path to its comforting conclusion in platitude. This interpretation permits us to describe the function of the characters more exactly and assert that the Justice and Julia, however important their presence, cannot be given more lines since they would then be expressing matters which must be reserved for the main characters. Given the peculiar status of the bawds it is essential for Mistress Overdone to express mercy and sympathy for Claudio and only then indignation at the effect the proclamation will have upon her trade. Lucio's bawdry, it will be shown, is equally appropriate to his character and function. The Duke's strange soliloquies are strange precisely because they must be recognized as marks of important change. The confusions of the night at the prison are, in part, a clear expression of the struggle between the Duke and Angelo in which the rule of law is only with difficulty established over the machinations of tyranny. It gives us, in other words, good reason for believing that the shape and form of the play is the result of deliberate design—design that went as far as to provide the double division of the play into eight and eight and ten and six expressing the crisis of justice, grace and mercy which will finally reduce the eight characters who mainly act out the question of justice into four married couples—the symbol of harmony and the number of concord.

3 Shakespeare's Comic Method

In order, therefore to appreciate the nature of this artistic triumph and understand the problems which it poses its audience the play must be seen not as some dark aberration but as a normal and crucial stage in Shakespeare's development.

The enormous technical triumphs of *Julius Caesar* and *Hamlet* made possible, after 1599, the power and intensity of the great tragedies. It may be possible to speak of a tragic period but it would be a mistake to regard these plays as evidence of a despairing spirit or consider the comedies written at the same time as inevitably tinged with pessimism. The early comedies contain matter dark enough for any melancholic taste. Their range of thought and emotion is astonishing and the reaction of an audience to *A Midsummer Night's Dream* or *Twelfth Night* may be as highly charged as their response to *King Lear*. Both kinds of play illumine the strong bonds of human affection and its power to transform existence even in the face of death. Shakespeare never stopped writing comedy and the plays produced during this great central period are both an independent triumph and the logical connection between the early romantic successes and the last great comic sequence on the triumph of time, composed between 1608 and 1611, which contains *Pericles*, *Cymbeline*, *The Winter's Tale* and *The Tempest*, arguably the finest plays he ever wrote.

The central comedies, *Troilus and Cressida*, *All's Well That Ends Well*, and *Measure for Measure* can properly be grouped together because they share a form of construction and a method of manipulating comic convention which differs radically from Shakespeare's normal practice. It is an old principle that the art of the drama is the art of preparation. Compression of time, and the short span of human attention, compel a playwright to provide his audience with continuous predictions of what is about to happen on stage, as well as information about the action actually taking place. This structure of information and prediction is one of the most vital elements in any plot. It is said that at the first performance of *The Importance of Being Earnest* Oscar Wilde paced backstage in an agony of apprehension until the moment when Jack enters in mourning for his brother Ernest. The audience have to appreciate that not only is Ernest a fiction but that he is a fiction who is at that very instant being successfully impersonated by Algernon captivating Cecily in the next room. The roar of laughter which greeted Jack's entrance was, therefore, sufficient indication to the author that his preparation had been successful. It is also a perfect example of the operation of incongruent information—that is, information which is known to the audience but is not shared in equal measure by the characters on stage. A character performs within a known situation but the acts and words that he considers appropriate may have another significance to an audience able to place them in a totally different context. Tragic irony is evidently one kind of incongruent information but it also forms the constant pattern of comedy.

In an excellent and important book, *Shakespeare's Comedies*, Bertrand Evans showed that Shakespeare used incongruent information (which he calls 'discrepancy of awareness') as his basic structural principle in the creation of comedy.[6] At a fairly simple level *The Comedy of Errors* depends upon the audience, but not the characters, knowing that there are two sets of identical twins within the city of Ephesus. In *Love's Labour's Lost* the comic complication depends on the incongruity of the information possessed by the Lords, the Ladies, the Pedants and the Clowns. In *A Midsummer Night's Dream* the lovers and mechanicals pick their way with partial sight through the coils of the wood near Athens, made even more puzzling by Puck's misapplication of love-in-idleness, to a resolution which still leaves them unaware of the beneficent fairy power imperfectly controlling their fates. As play succeeds play a distinct and recognizable pattern develops. The character who possesses the greatest amount of accurate information, and can therefore use it to manipulate the other characters, is the heroine. As Evans expresses it: 'The heroines of Shakespeare's comedies either hold from the outset, or very shortly gain, the highest vantage-point in their worlds.'[7] This is evidently true of *The Two Gentlemen of Verona*, *Much Ado About Nothing*, *The Merchant of Venice*, *As You Like It* and *Twelfth Night*.

This statement is, in effect, a key to the nature of early Shakespearean comedy. These naturally masterful and controlling heroines invariably fall in love. Their avowed aim is to realize this love in action and their purposes are therefore usually benevolent. This good will extends throughout the action of the play and it therefore follows that the anxieties aroused by the details of the story—as Shylock's pound of

[6] Bertrand Evans, *Shakespeare's Comedies* (Oxford 1960).
[7] *Shakespeare's Comedies*, 15–16.

flesh—are all successfully contained within this context of universal reassurance. The Forest of Arden turns out to be as enchanted as the wood near Athens, Venice and Verona belong to that Italy of the heart's desire where all ends well. What Shakespeare did with this brilliantly enchanted world (which was also a clear commercial success) was to shatter it to bits and attempt to rebuild it, not nearer the heart's desire, but nearer that truth of constraining circumstance which must limit all earthly paradises. The great triumph of the central comedies is to accomplish this transition from the world of fairy tale to the world of romance where love and beauty will endure both the tale that is told in winter and the shipwreck of the tempest. It is, therefore, significant that Evans's brilliant description of Proteus in *The Two Gentlemen of Verona* is as applicable to Angelo as it is to Leontes: 'The case of Proteus, hero bent on making a villain of himself, is typical: in the comedies villainy can but peep at what it would, for it is circumscribed and rendered impotent, if not ridiculous, by the bright-eyed heroines who, with their superior awareness, control everything in this woman's world.'[8] What has changed is the degree of control exercised by the heroines. It is not a change in the nature of the girls, since Isabella, Helena, Imogen or Perdita are as interesting as Julia, Portia, Rosalind or Viola. The way in which Shakespeare altered their circumstances in the central comedies is by changing the way in which he kept his audience informed of the situation.

What Professor Evans has established is that, in the early comedies, as much information is given to the audience as early as possible. They, therefore, make up their minds about most of the main characters from an early stage and there is little that can occur to shake their faith in Portia or Rosalind. This is not true of *Measure for Measure*. Here information given after the event must cause a radical revision of the audience's estimate of a character. The Duke's disguise at first appears as the normal operation of incongruent information. No firm reason, however, is offered for his appointment of Angelo and the justification for that strange decision only emerges in the course of the action. Angelo himself is unlike the Duke's first description of him—not merely because of his attempted rape of Isabella but because of the rejection of Mariana. This vital clue to his personality is only released half way through the play.

Equally important is the treatment of Isabella. At the time that her virginity is required of her there is no suggestion that the sacrifice would be futile. The audience watch Isabella's interview with Claudio without any awareness that the compromise he asks is impossible since Angelo

[8] *Shakespeare's Comedies*, 17.

will execute him in any case. Nor is there any precedent in the early comedies for the way in which the clowns and characters of 'low life' are here allowed to win two major dramatic victories over the main characters before they are controlled in the final reconciliation which many critics have felt to be less than conclusive. It appears that the doubts, hesitations and provisional judgements which are such a feature of criticism of the play have their origin within its dramatic structure. It is a comedy of delayed interpretation.

This delay, I believe, is Shakespeare's method of dramatizing moral questions, the ambiguity of action and the uncertainty of choice —without losing the basic advantage of a comic structure. The heroines of the romantic comedies are not only in control of their worlds —they are by far the best and brightest people in them. The consummation of their love is devoutly wished for by both spectators and characters. The moral position is not in doubt—indeed some of the difficulties that we now experience with *The Merchant of Venice* may be due to the play's apparent failure to question its assumed convention of Christian virtue. *Julius Caesar* brings such certainty to an end. There the spectator may hope for the conspiracy's success and yet be appalled by it. Antony wins sympathy in the market place with his genuine love for Caesar at the same time as he arouses revulsion by using that love as a calculated instrument of policy. Even Cassius commands respect and understanding as he is overwhelmed by the monster he has himself created, a politic plot which can only be led by Brutus, a man incapable of successful conspiracy. The clash of swords dramatizes the opposition of claims which are both valid and irreconcilable. No one steps forward to tell the audience what they should think and feel. In the comedies there is no need; in the plays after *Julius Caesar* there is no point. They are designed to provoke opposing reactions. To make up one's mind about the characters in a Shakespeare play is to find one's own position in some of the great moral and political debates which have extended from the Renaissance to our own time and which our successors are likely to keep alive. *Measure for Measure* clearly dramatizes exactly such a divisive debate.

4 The Historical Setting

It is probably the first play Shakespeare wrote in the reign of King James VI and I. The new king had taken Shakespeare's company under his own protection and there is evidence that the dramatist had considered the taste and opinions of his royal patron very carefully. Indeed some critics believe that in striving to content the king, Shakespeare has been driven to include in his comedy things which can never please. Yet any consideration of the opposition of Angelo and Isabella, and its resolution through the intervention of Mariana under the guidance of the Duke, must emphasize how far the leading dramatist of the King's Men has gone beyond mere compliment and entertainment. Other courtly pageants of the year 1604 have faded and left no wrack behind. *Measure for Measure* remains to puzzle the will. Shakespeare was capable of handling its themes of justice, charity and government in a fashion undreamt of in the philosophy of James and therefore his play still proves in performance to be a dazzling theatrical device for disturbing the intellect and delighting the imagination.

The opening of the play draws attention to its proposed subject. Handing over his power, the Duke modestly declines to instruct Escalus:

> Of government the properties to unfold
> Would seem in me t'affect speech and discourse,
> Since I am put to know that your own science
> Exceeds, in that, the lists of all advice
> My strength can give you: (I.i.3–7)

The Duke is one of the chief instruments used by the dramatist to unfold the art of government in his fictional Vienna to an audience. The disclaimer is instructive since James rated highly his own grasp of the arts of government. In 1598 the king had composed for his eldest son, Prince Henry, a treatise which he called *Basilicon Doron* (a title transliterated from Greek meaning 'The Kingly Gift'). This had been privately printed in 1599 in Scotland and in 1603, on James's accession to the English throne, it was published in London.

Louis Albrecht and David Lloyd Stevenson have drawn attention to a number of obvious similarities between the political philosophy of *Basilicon Doron* and the thought and conduct of the Duke in *Measure for Measure*.[9] Like James, the Duke believes that a ruler ought himself to be a pattern of virtue, and that those virtues must, if they are to be of any value, be expressed in action. Such actions expose a ruler to the risk of misrepresentation and slander which the Duke, like the king, regards as one of the most detestable of crimes. The opinions of the Duke on mercy, justice, and the necessity of firm government can all be paralleled in the treatise. Professor Stevenson concludes his examination of the evidence in this way:

> Duke Vincentio, though he has been variously identified by contemporary scholars as a stock character in Jacobean comedy and as a forebear of Prospero, in *The Tempest*, is also, and much more importantly, seen to be the figure of a Renaissance prince and autocrat, wilfully Jamesian in his views of himself and in his attitudes toward affairs of state. We are forced to conclude that Shakespeare's intentions were deliberate, that he created in the Duke a character whose acts and whose theories of government would be interesting to the new age and its new king because they were so carefully like ones which the king had identified as his own.[10]

In a further important study Josephine Waters Bennett has argued that the play was not only written with the king in mind, it was specifically commissioned to open the Christmas celebrations on St Stephen's night, 26 December 1604, the first Christmas which James had kept in London at Whitehall.[11] There exists an extract from the accounts of the Master of the Revels which records such a performance and which is now generally accepted as genuine. There are also, as Professor Bennett points out, a number of specific references in the play to members of the court who might be expected to be present at the performance on St Stephen's night. At II.iv.78–81 the lines:

> Thus wisdom wishes to appear most bright
> When it doth tax itself: as these black masks
> Proclaim an enshielded beauty ten times louder
> Than beauty could, display'd.

[9] L. Albrecht, *Neue Untersuchungen zu Shakespeares Mass für Mass* (Berlin 1914) and D. L. Stevenson, *The Achievement of Shakespeare's Measure for Measure'* (Ithaca, N.Y. 1966).

[10] *The Achievement of Shakespeare's 'Measure for Measure'*, 162.

[11] J. W. Bennett, *'Measure for Measure' as Royal Entertainment* (New York 1966).

probably refer to Ben Jonson's *Masque of Blackness* in which the queen and eleven of her ladies were to appear as 'blackamoors' in the closing performance of the festivities on Twelfth Night, 6 January 1605.

The second scene of the first act begins with this exchange:

> *Lucio:* If the Duke, with the other dukes, come not to composition with the King of Hungary, why then all the dukes fall upon the King.
>
> *Gent.:* Heaven grant us its peace, but not the King of Hungary's:

The queen's brother, the duke of Holstein, had come to England in November 1604 to raise men for a force he planned to take to Hungary. There a long war had been in progress since 1593. It was a confused three-cornered struggle between the Emperor Rudolf II, one of whose titles was king of Hungary, the Turks, the Protestant province of Transylvania and Michael of Moldavia. Transylvania had been reduced by the imperial general George Basta in August 1604 and a reign of terror followed. At Christmas 1604 the king of Hungary's peace would have a particularly menacing meaning and, since the duke of Holstein remained in England till June 1605, it is probable that he would have been present at the performance.

The other court figure clearly referred to is the king himself. In 1776 Thomas Tyrwhitt pointed out that two passages, the Duke's abrupt leave-taking at I.i.68–73 and Angelo's soliloquy at II.iv.24, reflect tactfully on the discomfort James felt at the pressing eagerness of his English subjects to catch a glimpse of their new king. D. L. Stevenson quotes the account by Gilbert Dugdale in *The Time Triumphant* (1604) to show that these passages must refer to James.[12] The king took coach to the Exchange in order to view the decorations and triumphal arches prepared for the royal procession to the coronation at Westminster. There he was so pressed in upon by the populace that he had to take refuge in the Exchange and have the doors closed.

These clear references, and many other features of the play, led Professor Bennett to her conclusion that the play was specifically written for the Christmas of 1604. The assembled evidence is not sufficient to make such a hypothesis certain but it is evident, beyond any reasonable doubt, that the accession of James had a profound influence upon the writing of *Measure for Measure*. It was composed at a moment that Gilbert Dugdale, and many others, obviously regarded as a time triumphant. The new reign was greeted with hope and optimism which perhaps gave an added sincerity to the traditional images of official pageantry appropriate to such an occasion. There are few better examples of this symbolism than

[12] *The Achievement of Shakespeare's 'Measure for Measure'*, 140–41.

the arches of triumph which James had hoped to see when he was mobbed at the Exchange. We have accounts of them by Stephen Harrison, the joiner and architect who was responsible for their construction, and by Thomas Dekker and Ben Jonson who were responsible for the poetic allegories incorporated within them. The sixth of these arches, erected 'above the conduit in Fleet Street', is described by Dekker as having, among other figures: 'The principal and worthiest was Astraea [Justice] sitting aloft, as being newly descended from heaven gloriously attired; all her garments being thickly strewed with stars, a crown of stars on her head, a silver veil covering her eyes.'[13] Under her were Virtue and Fortune with Envy occupying a dark and obscure place by herself. Below them were the four moral virtues opposite personifications of the four kingdoms now thought to be united under one rule—England, Scotland, France and Ireland. The whole arch, Dekker tells us, represents the moment written of by Virgil:

Iam redit et Virgo, redeunt Saturnia regna. (*Eclogues* IV.5)[14]

The virgin who returns is Astraea, daughter of the Titan Astraeus and the Dawn, who distributed justice among men during the golden age but was forced to retire from the earth during the age of iron and become the constellation Virgo. In 1603–4 it was a common compliment to say that the king, in uniting the kingdoms, was producing a union of peace and virtue that inaugurated a new golden age.

Ben Jonson, who shared with Dekker the responsibility for the triumphal arches, makes use of similar, but more elaborate, symbolism for his first two court masques. *The Masque of Blackness*, as we have seen, was performed at court on Twelfth Night 1605. *The Masque of Beauty*, its sequel, was not performed until 1608 but it shares a common inspiration. The 'blackamoors' portrayed by the queen and her ladies were the daughters of Niger who had been turned black by the sun. In brief, they arrive at the court of the sun-king James who is even more powerful than the celestial body since his power can turn them white, which was, for Jonson's purposes, equated with beauty. One of the most spectacular effects of the second masque was the arrival of the throne of beauty divided into eight squares with the sixteen masquers placed by couples within them. Jonson intended more than a simple compliment to the king. As Professor D. J. Gordon has written: 'More is involved here than the formal stereotyped gesture of the panegyrist; we are dealing here

[13] John Nichols, *The Progresses, Processions, and Magnificent Festivities of King James The First* (London 1828) vol. I, 369.
[14] Now returns the Virgin, now return the ages of Saturn.

with notions more "remov'd" than the everyday apotheosis of the Crown. A grander apotheosis is adumbrated, in which James is given the position and function assigned to the Sun in the theory of Beauty held by the Florentine Platonists.'[15]

Jonson was later to make clear his view that Shakespeare was not a learned dramatist. Yet it seems probable that the dramatist of the company most favoured by the court should know something of the style of compliment so lavishly expended at it. It was, I believe, exactly this familiarity which led him to write a play about the trials of a just virgin. Those trials, the condemnation of her brother and her own threatened rape, illuminate in many ways the promises and engagements entered into on betrothal and marriage. They also provoke a debate about licence and liberty, love and grace, justice and mercy in the government of a state which continues throughout the action. In resolving these difficulties by the union of justice and mercy in the proposed marriage of the Duke and Isabella Shakespeare found a way of complimenting his sovereign and engaging his interest in questions which deeply concerned both prince and people without offending against the strict stage censorship of the time. The play can be taken as expressing the confident hope that the new reign will be an age of measure for measure.

As can be seen from the accounts of Dugdale, Harrison, Dekker and Jonson, the arrival of the king in London was treated as a festival and triumph. The Renaissance had adapted the honour awarded by the senate of republican Rome—permission for an unusually successful general to march his troops through the city together with the prisoners and plunder taken during the campaign—for its own court ceremonial. The form was, therefore, used for both practical and literary purposes since it admitted exactly the kind of allegorical or symbolic references required on such occasions of high solemnity.[16] It is interesting that the Duke, who is never named in the play, should be called Vincentio in the list of characters. If he leaves the city privately at the beginning of the play he does return in full triumphal ceremonial through the gates at its end. The name may well carry its Italian meaning of 'conqueror'—the person most fitted to have a triumph. The clown, who is depicted as one of the chief instruments of vice in Vienna, is called Pompey. This name is used for two significant jokes. At II.i.200–10 Escalus established that his name is Pompey Bum and comments that he is 'in the beastliest sense' Pompey the

[15] D. J. Gordon, 'The Masque of Blacknesse and The Masque of Beautie', Journal of the Warburg and Courtauld Institutes, 6 (1943), 122–41.

[16] Alastair Fowler, Triumphal Forms (Cambridge 1970).

Great. Lucio repeats the joke at III.ii.40 when Pompey is being carried to prison:

> How now, noble Pompey! What, at the wheels of Caesar?
> Art thou led in triumph?

The Caesar on this occasion is Elbow, the Duke's constable. The combination of a head of state called Vincentio, an Elbow, and a bum or arse end of the commonwealth whose filthy habits must be reformed looks like a comic glance at the traditional theory of the state as a 'body politic'. The idea may have come from *Basilicon Doron* where the king writes: 'For ye shall make all your reformations to begin at your elbow, and so by degrees to flow to the extremities of the land.' (p. 85.) Vincentio does triumph over vice, and he triumphs over Angelo, the deputy who turned out to be considerably lower than the angels, but most of all he triumphs in restoring the righteous virgin who withstood both vice and tyranny. In the final union of justice and mercy the Duke brings to the body politic of Vienna the order and harmony which prevail in the macrocosm of God's universe. He has succeeded in making measure answer to measure.

There is no doubt that Shakespeare was thoroughly familiar with the Renaissance concept of a triumph since the King of Navarre's opening speech in *Love's Labour's Lost* celebrates the triumph of Fame. Jonson makes use of the same concept in *The Masque of Queens* (1609) and gives Cesare Ripa's *Iconologia* as his authority. Now, as D. D. Carnicelli has demonstrated, Ripa had drawn heavily on Renaissance representations of Petrarch's *Trionfi*—a poem that was considered his most powerful work until nearly the end of the sixteenth century.[17] Whether Shakespeare or Jonson knew Petrarch's poem is uncertain. They were certainly working in a tradition which derived from it. The *Trionfi* is a kind of allegorical or spiritualized autobiography which uses the imagery of a triumphal procession to mark six states of the human condition. The respective triumphs are, in order, those of Love, Chastity, Death, Fame, Time and Eternity. Love conquers all, reducing everything to its service but is unable to triumph over chastity. In turn chastity must yield to death but fame, or good reputation, can outlast death until defeated by time which will in the end bring all to oblivion—were it not for the fact that time itself must come to an end with the Day of Judgement when all the virtues become one in the triumph of God's eternity. Although not slavishly followed, this triumphal progression exists in *Measure for*

[17] D. D. Carnicelli, *Lord Morley's Tryumphes of Fraunces Petrarcke: The First English Translation of the 'Trionfi'* (Cambridge, Mass. 1971), 67.

Measure. Lucio, Claudio and all Vienna are in thrall to love. Only Angelo in his virtue appears to hold out and it is for this reason that the Duke chooses him to cleanse Vienna of its lechery. Angelo, however, falls a victim to love and, as lust's servant, is resisted by the chaste Isabella. The deputy overcomes her chastity by threatening the life of her brother, and actually thinks he has killed him. He hopes to cover this crime by the strength of his own reputation and the question debated before the Duke is whether he or Isabella should be believed. It is relevant that at this point Angelo should be shown as having reduced himself below the level of the slanderer Lucio whose vices he should have suppressed and curbed. The return of the Duke in deliberately staged triumph eventually assures the victory of Isabella's reputation while the revelation of Angelo's crimes certainly threatens to bring him to oblivion and death. Time, however, also reveals that Claudio is alive and the final union of justice and mercy proclaims the final triumph of eternal grace. Isabella pleads for Angelo and the lust which nearly consumed Vienna is transmuted into the harmony of the promised marriages.

A play which ends with a triumph of eternity might indeed be thought to assert that measure answers to measure—or, if not, then the fault should be looked for in us or in our changed circumstances. It is here that Shakespeare demonstrates his brilliance as a dramatist and, arguably, his understanding of the Christian religion. It is precisely because of the triumph of eternity that measure cannot answer to measure. It is not surprising that this play should be filled with biblical quotations and overtly Christian concepts to an extent quite unusual in Shakespeare's plays. But the solution is not only in the words. The dramatist has built it into the very fabric of his play.

The relationship between grace and justice is clearly a suitable subject for a play performed before a king who had so recently been welcomed to his new kingdom with triumphant shows and festivities. Shakespeare adopted the subject, the language and the symbolism appropriate to such an occasion and fashioned them in to his own triumphal form which can certainly be read as an expression of hope that these virtues will be combined in the new government. It also reminds its audience of the difficulty of defining mercy and justice and the enormous effort required to unite them, amid the corrupted currents of this world, in the government of intractable humanity. England's first Stuart sovereigns failed to achieve the triumph of Duke Vincentio, indeed they so unbalanced the state that it cost Charles I his life. Shakespeare's choice of subject for the year 1604 is an illuminating one. The complex way in which it is handled, a plot in which measure never does quite answer to measure so that the gap between them has to be bridged by the grace of love, a grace whose operation may be called a mystery, accounts both for the play's difficulty and for its enduring achievement.

5 The Sources

The complexity of Shakespeare's treatment becomes apparent in the way he used his sources. When James arrived in England Shakespeare was finishing, or had just finished, *Othello*. This play must be dated before 1603 since the bad quarto of *Hamlet*, published in that year, contains phrases which the pirate had picked up from *Othello*. For that play Shakespeare found in Cinthio's *Hecatommithi* (1565) a story, that of Disdimona and the Moor, from which he could create his plot. The episode from which *Measure for Measure* proceeds was probably suggested to Shakespeare by his reading in the *Hecatommithi* the story which may be summarized in the following way.

Juriste, governor of Innsbruck, condemns the youthful Vico to death for rape. Epitia, Vico's sister, pleads for her brother's life. Juriste offers Vico's life in exchange for sexual intercourse with Epitia. She consents, but Vico is executed despite her compliance. Juriste then adds sadism to sexuality by sending Epitia the head and body of her dead brother. She appeals for justice to the Emperor Maximinian. He orders Juriste to marry her, to clear her reputation from the stain of fornication, and then condemns him to execution. Epitia, however, now pleads so earnestly for the life of her new husband that the Emperor is moved to spare him.

Just before his death in 1573, Cinthio dramatized the story in a play called *Epitia*—which remained unprinted until given to the press by his son in 1583. To suit this different form, Cinthio considerably modified the story. Juriste condemns Vico to death for raping a virgin. Epitia pleads as before for her brother's life. In this version she is well known to Juriste and he hopes to marry her. He proposes to exchange her brother's life for her virginity. She consents when he promises to justify the act by marrying her at some future date. Juriste also has a sister, Angela, who knows of the bargain and approves of Epitia's conduct. She feels herself dishonoured when Juriste persists in the execution of Vico after sleeping with Epitia. Again the head and body of her dead brother are sent to Epitia who appeals to the emperor. Angela is called as a witness. She agrees that Epitia has told the truth. The Emperor orders Juriste to marry Epitia. She is unwilling to do so but consents to the imperial decree, intending to leave her husband immediately. Juriste is now condemned to death and Angela pleads with Epitia to intercede for her brother. This she refuses to do—until she learns from the governor of the prison that he had freed Vico, who is still alive, and sent the head and body of a condemned criminal to Epitia. The Emperor, at Epitia's request, pardons Vico for the rape he committed and then, somewhat more reluctantly, yields to her entreaty to spare Juriste as well, after which she embraces him willingly as her husband.

During the action of the play there is some argument between a magistrate, who is urging Juriste that severity is necessary to maintain order, and Juriste's secretary who pleads on Vico's behalf. In some respects this discussion appears to anticipate that of Angelo and Escalus in *Measure for Measure*.

In 1578 George Whetstone published *Promos and Cassandra*, a two part play based on Cinthio's story. In 1582 he published a transcription of the play in novella form in his *Heptameron of Civill Discourses*. The main episodes from the ten acts of Whetstone's play may be summarized in this way.

The scene is laid in the city of Julio, part of the domain of Corvinus, king of Hungary and Bohemia. The governor of the city, Promos, condemns Andrugio to death for fornication—although he is prepared to make amends by marrying the girl, Polina. Cassandra, the sister of Andrugio, pleads before Promos for her brother's life. He has never seen her before but her presence arouses an uncontrollable sexual passion. In order to gratify this sudden lust he promises to spare her brother and marry her—upon condition that she yields her virginity to him instantly. She believes both promises and consents. However, even before he consummates his desire, Promos gives orders for Andrugio's execution. As in Cinthio's versions the girl now receives what she takes to be her brother's body and mangled head. She appeals to Corvinus who orders Promos to marry Cassandra and then instantly forfeit his own head. Cassandra now pleads for her husband's life. Corvinus remains unmoved until Andrugio, who had been released by the jailor and remained in hiding, presents himself before the king determined, at whatever risk to himself, to help his sister. Corvinus pardons him on condition that he marries Polina and, for Cassandra's sake, finally pardons Promos.

Round this main plot Whetstone deploys a good deal of material concerning low life in the city of Julio. Particular attention is paid to the efforts of Phallax, a factotum of Promos, to join forces with the courtesan Lamia and suppress their competitors engaged in prostitution and other usual forms of vice throughout the city. They too are dealt with during the King's visitation. Some slight changes in the method of disclosure adopted by Andrugio are found in Whetstone's prose version in his *Heptameron*. There, however, the whole story is reported by Madam Isabella—a name which Shakespeare seems to have adopted for his heroine.

That Shakespeare was acquainted with all of these versions seems probable. The most doubtful case is Cinthio's play *Epitia* and here there is a coincidence of the name Angelo—recalling Angela the governor's sister—while the handwriting and seal of the Duke which the disguised Friar shows the Provost in IV.ii recalls the letter in Juriste's hand and bearing his seal which the Podesta shows as his warrant for Vico's execution. Of those scholars who have recently concerned themselves with Shakespeare's sources, Professor Muir, having listed the parallels between *Epitia* and *Measure for Measure*, regards the argument for Shakespeare's knowledge of the play as a strong one while Professor Bullough regards Shakespeare's knowledge of Cinthio's drama as established.

In all of these versions of the story, Juriste and Promos have legal warrant for condemning the ravisher or fornicator to death, but then deprive themselves of any possible justification by their seduction of the condemned man's sister. This condemnation is particularly harsh in the later version since the boy is willing and eager to marry the girl. Only in Cinthio's initial version is the condemned man actually executed and his body really sent to his sister—all other versions leave him alive and substitute another corpse. Yet all versions insist that the governor has issued orders for the prisoner's execution, despite his promise and his exaction of sexual consummation from the boy's sister. Only in Shakespeare's version does the heroine refuse to yield her virginity in exchange for her brother's life.

It is evident that Shakespeare's English audience could not but regard the deputy's original decision—quite apart from his later criminal conduct—as unjustifiable. Even extreme Puritans, who regarded adultery as deserving the death penalty, did not hold fornication to be so serious a crime. Angelo's subsequent conduct makes clear his heartless nature and his determination to regard himself as above the law he administers. The moral of the older versions appears to be that the experience of being first bedded and then wedded is sufficiently powerful to overcome both the natural reluctance of the heroine and even her revulsion at having held her brother's headless body in her arms. The plea which the heroine utters for her husband's life may be presented as an act of Christian humility but it can also be interpreted as condoning, in prurient fashion, the violent and perverse conduct of the deputy. This opportunity for the moral enjoyment of sexual sadism no doubt accounts for the tale's popularity. It is Shakespeare's triumph to have totally changed the moral basis of the story without softening or weakening its nature. Isabella's refusal of Angelo's bargain necessitates the introduction of Mariana. Out of this necessity Shakespeare creates the opportunity for the extended examination of the mystery of love which lies at the heart of the play's complexity.

6 The Legal Question

One of the most important pieces of delayed information that the audience receives about Angelo is that he was once engaged to marry Mariana. It is here that the historian must help the director, actor or critic since Shakespeare naturally expected his audience to be familiar with contemporary marriage customs and they, like other fashions, are liable to change. The best and most accurate account of this matter is contained in an important article by Ernest Schanzer.[18] It is evident that some kind of contract existed between Angelo and Mariana in which they had promised to marry each other at a future date. This would normally be a *sponsalia de futuro* which could be dissolved, for good reason, by either of the parties. Angelo himself appears to treat it in this way when he claims (V.i.214–20) that it was broken off because of the loss of Mariana's dowry and her 'levity'. Mariana and the Duke both treat the contract as a more binding one—that of sworn spousals, *sponsalia iurata*, which could not be dissolved without the consent of both parties. When, therefore, Mariana takes Isabella's place in the bed within Angelo's summer house she is keeping her sworn oath and making Angelo keep his. By the custom of the time sexual consummation converts their sworn spousals into marriage. This kind of marriage contract was known as a contract *per verba de praesenti* and it plays a crucial part in the structure of *Measure for Measure*.

In 1563 the Council of Trent, that powerful instrument of the Counter-Reformation, ruled that marriage in states in obedience to the doctrines of Rome required the presence of a priest. The priest, however, was not there to administer the sacrament of marriage, for the man and woman entering upon matrimony were its ministers. The priest was present as a witness only—but his presence was essential for the marriage to have the binding force of a civil and religious contract. The Protestant countries of Europe still maintained the pre-Tridentine tradition. A pledge or declaration of marriage, made before witnesses, constituted a valid and legal marriage. It was not necessary for the witnesses to be ministers of the

[18] Ernest Schanzer, 'The Marriage-Contracts in *Measure for Measure*.' *Shakespeare Survey 13* ed. Allardyce Nicoll (Cambridge 1960), 81–9.

Church. In 1604 such a contract was binding in all of the countries ruled by King James—and it remained a legal form of marriage in Scotland until 1939. The jurist Henry Swinburne, a contemporary of Shakespeare's whose book *A Treatise on Spousals* must have been written about 1600 although it was not published till 1686, held that the mutual acceptance of each other as husband and wife constituted marriage, even though no witnesses were present.

It is true that there was already a strong feeling, especially among the more puritanically minded, that the church ceremony should precede cohabitation. By 1613, when James's daughter Elizabeth was about to marry the Elector Palatine, Shakespeare made Prospero in *The Tempest* (one of the many pieces performed before the engaged pair) express similar views. The weight of parental and ecclesiastical disapproval had not, however, yet changed the law and in 1604 Shakespeare clearly expected his audience to have the laws of England in mind as they contemplated the sexual situation in his fictional Vienna. In this Vienna Claudio is condemned to death for fornication—a sin which the Church everywhere regarded as heinous and deadly, though not necessarily a capital offence. In Vienna Claudio clearly falls within the scope of the law.

Yet, as he informs Lucio and the audience, he regards himself as married to Juliet, the girl who now carries his child:

> Thus stands it with me: upon a true contract
> I got possession of Julietta's bed.
> You know the lady; she is fast my wife,
> Save that we do the denunciation lack
> Of outward order; this we came not to,
> Only for propogation of a dow'r
> Remaining in the coffer of her friends.
> From whom we thought it meet to hide our love
> Till time had made them for us. But it chances
> The stealth of our most mutual entertainment,
> With character too gross, is writ on Juliet.   (I.ii.138–48)

The fact that they concealed their love until Juliet's friends were won over and prepared to pay her dowry has brought him within the letter of the law. The fact that he is, *per verba de praesenti*, married to Juliet leads him to think that he is condemned, as he says 'for a name' and gives him hope that his sister may be able to plead with the deputy. It is here that Shakespeare makes skilful use of what we have called incongruent information.

The fact that Claudio is married is now known to the audience. It is not known to Isabella. This is made clear by her first reaction to the news of Juliet's pregnancy, 'O, let him marry her!' (I.iv.49.) It is, therefore, ironic that Isabella has to plead for Claudio believing him to be guilty of fornication, 'a vice that most I do abhor' (II.ii.29), and is thus forced to plead only on the strong compulsion that he is her brother. In dramatic terms this device is essential. Shakespeare has ensured the full sympathy of his audience for Claudio, but it would be an enormous loss in tension if the crucial scenes between Angelo and Isabella should turn upon a legal quibble instead of the question that Shakespeare had proposed, Angelo's rigid adherence to the letter of the law and Isabella's appeal for mercy and grace. This appeal provokes Angelo's attempted rape, an act which leaves him in exactly the same situation for which he had condemned Claudio, married on a *de praesenti* contract which is this time so secret that he himself is as yet unaware of it. Since, however, it is the result of his own sworn spousals his ignorance of the act he has actually committed does not invalidate the marriage.

Angelo is thus trapped by the very letter of the law he had served with such severity. He is freed by the spirit which he had not only denied but had attempted to corrupt when he recognized it in Isabella. The torchbearer of grace on this occasion is clearly Mariana. Like the heroines of the early comedies, what she has in view is the realization of her love. In the light of that passion it is possible to see Angelo's act in the summer house in two opposed ways. The taking of Isabella's virginity would be an act of forced fornication amounting to rape. In taking Mariana's Angelo unknowingly performs an act of love which, in the end, saves him not only from death but from the cruelty of his own nature. This transformation of the acts of man, so that sinful actions have good consequences, is the operation of grace. It is possible that Shakespeare had in mind St Paul's great comparison of the law and the gospel in the second Epistle to the Corinthians where he talks of the epistle:

> written not with ink, but with the Spirit of the living God; not in tables of stone, but in fleshy tables of the heart. (II Cor. 3.3)

and where the ministers of the New Testament are emphatically declared to be ministers:

> not of the letter, but of the spirit: for the letter killeth, but the spirit giveth life. (II Cor. 3.6)

Certainly his use of the marriage contracts in *Measure for Measure* dramatizes very clearly the differences between the letter, which would literally result in the execution of Claudio and Angelo, and the spirit introduced by Mariana which gives life.

This contrast in the moral interpretation of a single physical act or person is continually employed by Shakespeare in the plays of this central period. Hamlet asks his mother to look upon the 'counterfeit presentment' of two brothers but the dramatist asks his audience to consider the act of killing, to compare the murder that is past with the murder that may yet come, in the dumb show and action of *The Murder of Gonzago*. The Helen of *Troilus and Cressida* may be the theme for honour and renown seen by Troilus or the whore that she is considered by Diomedes. Perhaps the most striking example comes in the final comedies though it may form part of the source material of *Measure for Measure*. In *Cymbeline* Imogen wakes to find the headless body of Cloten beside her and mistakes it for that of her husband Posthumus. She then judges as much by the outward show, and misses the spirit which gives life, as did Posthumus in believing Iachimo's report of her unfaithfulness. It seems that Shakespeare here at last found a use for the body sent to Epitia.

The double interpretation of people and their purposes runs right through *Measure for Measure* and is the source of the play's enormously disturbing power. Shakespeare's double structure celebrates the law and yet supersedes it by grace. The compliment to the king also reminds him of the difficulty of the duty he has to perform. The triumphal form celebrating good government and firm virtue involves virtue and government in a conflict which calls in question their nature and very existence. It perpetually reminds its audience not only that conventional wisdom and accepted morality form a thin layer arched over chaos, but that convention and accepted custom may not be the best way of dealing with the emerging tyranny of mankind's terrible passions. The difficulties encountered by the characters amid the courts and stews of Vienna mirror the problems of countless audiences in introducing any measure or harmony into their own lives. It speaks above all of the power of love and charity without which all time and measure is lost and the human instruments, of whatever race or creed, become the sounding brass or tinkling cymbal scorned by St Paul.

It is this complexity which has caused difficulty for critics and spectators who are determined to simplify and solve the problems of measure for measure in terms of their own elementary morality. Isabella must be either a saint or a sexual hysteric, the Duke must appear as God's deputy furthering the ways of providence or as a sly and incompetent machiavellian. Put in these crude terms it is evident that the descriptions are inadequate. It is impossible to do justice to the play in the kind of moral shorthand used by the Duchess in *Alice in Wonderland*. The problems of *Measure for Measure* remain to engage the emotions and trouble the intellect long after the play is over.

7 The Play

The beginning of the play now appears singularly effective. The reference to King James's dislike of crowds would have attracted, inevitably, the attention of its first audiences. It is such an odd reason for the Duke to offer that an actor should have no difficulty in capturing attention for the lines, even from those who know nothing of James or his views. It appears to give information—and yet it diverts attention from the fact that no real explanation is given for the Duke's action. Such a smokescreen is useful because the Duke's reasons are not the dramatist's—and the Duke is as yet unaware of the education that the drama has in store for him. That education will consist of the unfolding of the properties of government which he is too modest to disclose to Escalus. In this first scene, therefore, Shakespeare deliberately delays information that will allow his audience to understand the Duke. He also, in more remarkable fashion, focuses attention upon the information about Angelo which the audience must recognize when they finally hear it. In the light of later events the Duke's words of surrender must seem ironic:

> Angelo,
> There is a kind of character in thy life
> That to th'observer doth thy history
> Fully unfold. (I.i.27–30)

The Duke, it turns out, understands Angelo's real character well enough. He is presented to the audience as a puritan paragon for the moment in order to illuminate a very specific point. The Duke gives as one of his reasons for Angelo's elevation that:

> Heaven doth with us as we with torches do,
> Not light them for themselves; for if our virtues
> Did not go forth of us, 'twere all alike
> As if we had them not. (I.i.33–6)

When Milton wrote that he could not praise a fugitive and cloistered virtue he was simply giving classic expression to generations of Protestant belief. They interpreted the parable of the talents as clear evidence that virtue, like the other gifts of God, was intended for use rather than mere conservation.

The Duke, however, goes farther than this. He grants Angelo full powers:

> Mortality and mercy in Vienna
> Live in thy tongue and heart.   (I.i.45–6)

and he repeats the point immediately before camouflaging his own exit with his dislike of pressing crowds and theatrical ceremonial:

>   your scope is as mine own,
> So to enforce or qualify the laws
> As to your soul seems good.,   (I.i.65–7)

The contrast between mortality and mercy or enforcement and qualification is bound to be noticed even at this early stage of the play. Insisted upon by every method open to the dramatist, it is not meant to escape the attention of the audience. It will become painfully evident that Angelo is unable, as the Duke's prescription requires, to unite his tongue and heart and give Vienna a true balance of mortality and mercy. The pressures of government reveal him to be a character fatally divided against himself. Yet in delivering this power to Angelo, the Duke admits that he believes himself incapable of uniting his own tongue and heart. That union is the subject of Shakespeare's play.

The next scene provides an enormous amount of information which advances the plot with the utmost rapidity. It opens with the conversation between Lucio and his friends which indirectly compliments the duke of Holstein. There were many in England who hoped that the advent of a sovereign from Calvinist Scotland would align their country more firmly with the Protestant forces of Europe. The 'action' that is referred to seemed a real possibility in 1604. From war their conversation naturally turns to love—but again it is an aspect of love that was peculiarly painful in seventeenth-century Europe. The jokes about 'three pil'd piece' and 'French velvet' were not then obscure. They refer to the progressive symptoms of syphilis, which had then become so virulent that it seemed as if some totally new disease had struck. It is not accidental that it is in this atmosphere, charged with jokes about a frightening sexually transmitted disease of the human body, that the audience first hears of Angelo's attempt by law and proclamation to cure the diseases of the body politic. It appears that Angelo's remedy is radical surgery—execution.

It is clear that those who regard courtly pursuits as the employment of their swords or their sexual organs are out of place in this new commonwealth. The ungentle Mistress Overdone and her tapster Pompey are equally misplaced. Their first conversation refers to the pulling down of brothels throughout Vienna. It is possible that the 'houses in the suburbs' could be a reference to the theatres. The accession of James resolved a situation for the theatres which had existed since 1597. Then, after a politically scandalous performance of *The Isle of Dogs*, the Privy Council had yielded to a petition from the City and ordered the destruction of all theatres in or about London. The new reign regularized the position of at least some of the companies. The matter would not be important unless it indicated that the dramatist expected his audience to sympathize, at least to some extent, with the situation of the bawds and vagabonds—since the Puritan government of the City of London tended to class actors in that company.[19]

This sympathy is strongly reinforced by the appearance of Claudio, led in triumph by the Provost to prison. This is the first deployment of the marriage contracts in the play. Claudio's declaration to Lucio, 'You know the lady, she is fast my wife' (I.ii.140), cannot fail to win sympathy. He begs Lucio to ask for help from his sister, due that day to take her vows as a novice at the convent of St Clare. He believes that:

> in her youth
> There is a prone and speechless dialect
> Such as move men; beside, she hath prosperous art
> When she will play with reason and discourse,
> And well she can persuade. (I.ii.175-9)

This speech prepares the way for one of the fundamental ironies of the play, one which must grip the audience as it slowly receives the necessary information. Claudio expects the language of the body, the simple fact of Isabella's youth and beauty, to plead his case more eloquently than reason. He is correct, but he had not allowed for the strange dialectic of passion which this appeal will arouse in the Deputy, nor is he ready to face the consequences. He has unwittingly set in motion the events which will lead to his terrible interview with his sister in the prison. If the price of life is Isabella's virginity then Claudio seems already prepared to pay it.

His appeal to Isabella and to Angelo has to be made through Lucio. This character gains in stature both in the way he responds to Claudio's appeal and in his gentle approach to the girl about to enter the convent. It is an important dramatic effect that the audience should first encounter Lucio as the witty winner of word games and also as a sincere and honest

[19] Glynne Wickham, *Early English Stages* (London 1972) Vol. II, part 2, 9-29.

friend. He will not retain all of this sympathy as the play progresses—nor
will his later palpable lies ever quite destroy his first reputation with an
audience for honest plain speaking. The concentrated interview between
the Duke and Friar Thomas comes between Lucio's interview with
Claudio and the summoning of Isabella. This scene establishes the Duke's
intention to visit both prince and people—but it also offers the audience
more information about the Duke which they will only understand at a
later stage of the action. He opens the scene by defending himself against
the charge that he is in love:

> No, holy father, throw away that thought;
> Believe not that the dribbling dart of love
> Can pierce a complete bosom.   (I.iii.1–3)

'Dribbling' is an odd word. It seems to be the same as the one used by
Sidney in the second sonnet of *Astrophil and Stella*:

> Not at first sight, nor with a dribbed shot
> Love gave the wound, which while I breathe will bleed
> But known worth did in mine of time proceed,
> Till by degrees it had full conquest got.

Sidney's most recent editor argues that the word must mean 'random'[20]
and that, I believe, is what it meant for Shakespeare and his Duke. He
does not expect that so complete a man as himself can be affected by the
random effects of love—an illusion which he shares with his appointed
deputy Angelo.

The Duke clearly expects a 'complete' man to be one of a sober and
stoical cast. His version, therefore, is singularly lacking in one of the
attributes of the figure of the courtier, scholar and soldier which Sidney
himself exemplified and which Shakespeare continually created
throughout his comedies and tragedies. Such a man would unite within
himself the power to pursue the active, the contemplative and the
passionate life. He would be as well-versed in the varieties of courtship as
in the scruples of philosophy and as adept at making love as he was
capable of making war. If the Duke is really proof against love then he is
not a complete man and, like so many self-praisers in Shakespeare's plays,
he turns out not to possess the quality which he holds up for admiration in
the mirror of his own vanity.

The point is important because the idea of the complete human
personality, a man capable of pursuing the active, the contemplative and
the passionate life is crucial for *Measure for Measure*. It sums up the entire

[20] W. A. Ringler, ed., *The Poems of Sir Philip Sidney* (Oxford 1962), 459.

philosophy of balance and correspondence on which the play is founded. The Duke's assertion that he is impervious to the passionate life is followed by an admission that a failure in his role as duke is causing him, temporarily, to withdraw to the more contemplative role of friar. He leaves Angelo to supply his place. When Friar Thomas objects that it would be more fitting for the Duke to enforce the laws himself he receives the interesting reply:

> Sith 'twas my fault to give the people scope,
> 'Twould be my tyranny to strike and gall them
> For what I bid them do; for we bid this be done,
> When evil deeds have their permissive pass
> And not the punishment.   (I.iii.35–9)

The Duke thinks of government in terms of horsemanship. He has already referred to the laws as 'The needful bits and curbs to headstrong steeds.' (I.iii.20.) He has to grant that having failed to put the harness of the state to its proper use he would now appear as a bad rider who strikes his horse for obeying his own mismanagement. Angelo, a man well known for the contemplative virtues, has therefore been chosen.

The Duke could now appear as a man determined to have unpopular measures performed by a severe, efficient, but disposable subordinate. This course is praised by Machiavelli in *The Prince*, but it was an old tradition by the time human affairs came under his scrutiny. The Duke contradicts such a view of his conduct by making plain his intention to visit both prince and people. His brief character sketch of Angelo makes it probable that the prince will be in greater need of visitation. The portrait of Angelo given by the Duke to Friar Thomas turns out to be a genuine mirror for magistrates, it reflects equally upon the character of the Duke:

>   Lord Angelo is precise;
> Stands at a guard with envy; scarce confesses
> That his blood flows, or that his appetite
> Is more to bread than stone. Hence shall we see,
> If power change purpose, what our seemers be.   (I.iii.50–54)

The Duke complains that Angelo is 'precise'—a word which tends to be used of those following the letter of a strict moral code. He fails to acknowledge his own blood or passion and resembles those condemned (in St Matthew 7.9) for offering a stone to a son asking for bread. The virtues which have so far appeared in Angelo's precise life of contemplation are now to be tried in the active world of government—and the Duke implies that they will be found to be mere 'seeming' or false show. Yet in the process of visiting the prince and people of Vienna the Duke will himself receive necessary instruction in the proper balance of the active, contemplative and passionate life.

It is not accidental that the fourth scene should be set in that haven of the contemplative life, the convent of the sisterhood of St Clare. Isabella is introduced to the audience as a girl of a precise turn of mind who desires even sterner restraints upon the liberty of the nuns than those provided in the rule of the order. Lucio, the devotee of the passionate life, is so evidently out of place here that even he is abashed and feels forced to qualify the jests about virginity naturally provoked in a man of his temperament. He has come to summon Isabella back from the very threshold of the contemplative life in order to pursue the active business of pleading for her brother's life—an act which will involve both Angelo and herself in a storm of passion which neither can control.

The movement of the characters in these first four scenes is thus both formal and exact in terms of the idea of the tripartite life. The Duke leaves the active for the contemplative while denying the passionate. Angelo, (who is known to deny the passionate) leaves the contemplative for the active task of curbing passion. Lucio (who contemplates the active life of the soldier and jokes with his fellows about the passionate) brings Isabella from the contemplative to the active—pleading against Angelo's too 'passionate' condemnation of her brother for committing the 'passionate' act which has made Juliet pregnant. As the balance changes, so each one of these characters is revealed as somehow lacking in the true measure or harmony of the union of the graces which makes up a soul in tune with the grace of God.

In the first four scenes only one character is aware that he has failed to maintain true measure in his life and he speaks with the bitter self-knowledge that all the others must taste before harmony can be restored to the body politic of Vienna

> *Lucio:* Why, how now, Claudio, whence comes this restraint?
> *Claudio:* From too much liberty, my Lucio, liberty;
>   As surfeit is the father of much fast,
>   So every scope by the immoderate use
>   Turns to restraint. Our natures do pursue,
>   Like rats that ravin down their proper bane,
>   A thirsty evil; and when we drink we die.   (I.ii.118–124)

In this extremity he hopes for help from the grace and mercy that he knows are in Isabella. Claudio is aware that he cannot save himself and that only his sister's qualities offer him hope of life. His prayer, however, cannot be answered until the stubborn pride of all the other characters has been humbled. Then they can acknowledge the 'thirsty evil' at work in their own lives, and can seek for grace. The religious implications of this are evident, but they should not lead to the conclusion that Shakespeare's triumphal form is a religious allegory. The play contains some of the elements that are associated with allegory; but is based upon moral and psychological observations whose continuing appeal depends upon the fact that men still believe them to be neither type nor symbol but simply true.

The second group of four scenes complete, as we have argued, the first 'measure' of the play concerned with the harsh operation of the law; the 'measure for measure' which Angelo offers to Isabella if she seeks to mitigate its severity. The action has evidently been moving towards the two major scenes between Angelo and Isabella. Their dramatic intensity is achieved as much by the context in which the interviews are placed as by the poetic power of argument. It is important that the scenes are separated from each other by the disguised Duke's conversation with Juliet, and that the whole group is introduced by the arraignment and abortive trial of Pompey and Froth at the suit of Elbow, the constable.

This is a scene which opens in deeply serious fashion. Escalus is still pleading for Claudio's life. He argues that if time, place and desire had coincided, then Angelo might have found himself in Claudio's situation. Angelo answers with one of the play's strongest speeches:

> 'Tis one thing to be tempted, Escalus,
> Another thing to fall. I not deny
> The jury, passing on the prisoner's life,
> May in the sworn twelve have a thief or two
> Guiltier than him they try. What's open made to justice,
> That justice seizes. What knows the laws
> That thieves do pass on thieves? 'Tis very pregnant,
> The jewel that we find, we stoop and take't,
> Because we see it; but what we do not see
> We tread upon and never think of it.
> You may not so extenuate his offence
> For I have had such faults; but rather tell me,
> When I, that censure him, do so offend,
> Let mine own judgement pattern out my death,
> And nothing come in partial. Sir, he must die.   (II.i.17–31)

In a most important article, A. D. Nuttall has argued that Angelo's attitude to the law must be considered tough-minded, intellectually respectable and morally defensible: 'Angelo grants at once that those who judge are not themselves free from sin. This may mean that they lack, at the metaphysical level, a "right" to judge, but it certainly does not mean that they cannot, at the practical level, do it.'[21]

Angelo's argument upholds the law. It makes the nature of the offence more important than the character of the criminal or the judge. It asserts the necessity of judging, even at the risk of being judged in one's own turn.

There is, however, a distinction to be made between the pragmatic acceptance of the jury service of sinners and the toleration of known criminals in the seats of judgement. It is consistent of Angelo to demand his own execution once he has been exposed by the Duke. It is tyrannous to use his power to gratify the lusts for which he kills Claudio. Law and government may be ruled by the practical and sometimes harsh necessities implied in Angelo's argument, but the rule of law is impossible when the governors are like Angelo, so inhumane as to be inhuman.

What follows provides a commentary on Angelo's speech. The constable leads in Froth and Pompey, 'two notorious benefactors'. Angelo corrects him, 'Are they not malefactors'—and receives a strange and confused reply:

> Elbow: If it please your honour, I know not well what they are; but precise villains they are, that I am sure of, and void of all profanation in the world that good Christians ought to have.   (II.i.52–5)

It is evident that nothing can be made open to justice through the fog of Elbow's 'misplacings'. Pompey takes advantage of this to conceal the whole matter under an amazing froth of words concerning Master Froth himself, the room at The Bunch of Grapes in which he was accustomed to sit, and the two prunes which were still standing in the good dish (though it was not a China dish) when Mistress Elbow came in and sat down because she was pregnant and had a craving for prunes. This brilliant narration has an extraordinary effect upon Angelo. It so wearies him that it drives him from the bench of justice. Pompey has here achieved an enormous triumph simply by the use of words. With Angelo on the bench they all stood in danger of their lives. His defeat at this point does not prove that he is a precise villain in whom the great power of office is misplaced—but it will surprise no one when he reveals that truth in the

[21] A. D. Nuttall, '*Measure for Measure*: Quid Pro Quo?' *Shakespeare Studies IV*, ed. J. Leeds Barroll (Cincinnati, Ohio 1968), 231–51.

next scene. Like the Duke, Angelo abdicates in the face of the stubborn resistance of the stews. He is then himself firmly hit by the 'dribbling dart of love'.

It is left to Escalus to moderate Pompey's triumph. This he does first by the important joke about 'Pompey the Great' and then by warning him against being a bawd—for Escalus has no doubt that he is one, although proof has so far eluded Constable Elbow. The exchange between them, however, is an important contribution to the debate about law in Vienna:

> *Pompey:* Truly, sir, I am a poor fellow that would live.
> *Escalus:* How would you live, Pompey—by being a bawd? What do you think of the trade, Pompey? Is it a lawful trade?
> *Pompey:* If the law would allow it, sir.
> *Escalus:* But the law will not allow it, Pompey; nor it shall not be allowed in Vienna.
> *Pompey:* Does your worship mean to geld and splay all the youth of the city?
> *Escalus:* No, Pompey.
> *Pompey:* Truly, sir, in my poor opinion, they will to't then. If your worship will take order for the drabs and the knaves, you need not to fear the bawds.
> *Escalus:* There is pretty orders beginning, I can tell you: It is but heading and hanging.   (II.i.211–25)

This remark strengthens the impression made by Escalus's appeal for Claudio at the beginning of the scene. He is doubtful about the excessive severity of the new order. Pompey proves himself a precisian in his neat interpretation of the law—since his trade would clearly be lawful if the law allowed it. The more serious question is then raised whether, in attempting to suppress the Vienna whore-houses by law, Angelo and the authorities are not engaged in a vain attempt to stifle one of the irrepressible laws of human nature. In bringing Pompey before the courts they are arraigning one of the parasites that feed upon human sexuality. In condemning Claudio for loving Juliet they are striking at one of the great bonds of society. The voice of low comedy has here an unchallengeable authority about the way in which measure actually answers to measure in the great business of the world.

The hints about the doubtfulness of Angelo's character, conveyed to the audience through the Duke, have now been supported by a most damaging, though not yet decisive, dramatic defeat. In the sustained brilliance of the next three scenes the audience watch the character of Angelo implode. The entire outer structure of the personality, the precise man of gravity whose personal abstinence is a source of doubt and fear, is carried away and he is nearly swept to destruction in the resulting firestorm of sexual passion.

The fifth scene ended with Escalus still grieving for the death of Claudio, for which he could see no remedy. The sixth scene opens with exactly the same sentiments expressed by the Provost:

> Alas,
> He hath but as offended in a dream!
> All sects, all ages, smack of this vice; and he
> To die for't!   (II.ii.4–6)

Within, therefore, a few minutes of each other two evidently worthy and honourable men give support (which he may not entirely deserve) to Pompey's case by their desire to help Claudio. Angelo is considerably handicapped by this weight of disapproval even before Isabella begins her plea. The established strength of his personality, and the philosophic power inherent in his mulish morality, must be gauged from the fact that, despite the odds in Isabella's favour, Angelo wins this first dramatic encounter.

Isabella leads with a clear exposition of her own feelings:

> There is a vice that most I do abhor,
> And most desire should meet the blow of justice;
> For which I would not plead, but that I must;
> For which I must not plead, but that I am
> At war 'twixt will and will not.   (II.ii.29–33)

In this instance she is compelled to regard the character rather than the crime since the author of vice is her own brother. Unaware of Claudio's regard for Juliet as 'fast my wife' she condemns him in her heart as a fornicator and can only plead for his life by making a distinction between the act and the actor:

> I have a brother is condemn'd to die;
> I do beseech you, let it be his fault,
> And not my brother.   (II.ii.34–6)

Angelo disposes of this apparent sophistry with contemptuous ease, 'Condemn the fault and not the actor of it!' but the edge of his intellect has missed the actual thread of Isabella's argument. Since he is her brother, she does not regard Claudio as a hardened fornicator properly deserving death. If he has committed the foul act of fornication it can only be as an isolated instance, and that instance should be condemned. If he is pardoned he will continue to be Claudio, but have ceased to be a fornicator, since the act will have died a well-deserved death. That this must be her meaning here is revealed by the fury with which she turns on her brother in the prison scene when he dares to ask her to exchange her chastity for his life. 'Thy sin's not accidental, but a trade.' (III.i.150.) This is an admission that Angelo was right. The actor becomes what his acts make him, the deed's creature.

At this stage it is plain that Isabella would herself have abandoned her appeal. It is Lucio who recalls her to her vocation of charity. His presence and participation in the scene emphasize the fundamental differences of thought and attitude which divide the characters. Angelo and Isabella both regard fornication as a deadly sin. The Provost and Lucio consider it as a natural, normal, or at least excusable part of ordinary behaviour. Isabella cannot adopt their attitude. Her continued advocacy, therefore, forces her to argue the case that the value and worth of the living individual is the paramount consideration and that this ought to outweigh whatever sins or crimes he may have committed. The fact that Claudio is her brother becomes the ground of her appeal, a man to whom Angelo, as to a brother in sin, ought to show mercy:

> *Isabella:* Must he needs die?
> *Angelo:*   Maiden, no remedy.
> Isabella: Yes; I do think that you might pardon him,
>   and neither heaven nor man grieve at the mercy.
> *Angelo:* I will not do't.
> *Isabella:*   But can you, if you would?
> *Angelo:* Look, what I will not, that I cannot do.
> *Isabella:* But might you do't, and do the world no wrong,
>   If so your heart were touch'd with that remorse
>   As mine is to him?   (II.ii.47–55)

Mercy becomes a ruler because it is a recognition, on his part, that in the criminal's place he would have offended too. Isabella is now dangerously close to arguing that the sin she most abhors is, in fact, so universal a fault that it can hardly deserve death. She never actually crosses that line, but her argument leads towards it. Angelo will force her to face that contradiction in the sharpest possible terms when he requires her virginity in exchange for his mercy.

Angelo takes his stand, as he had done with Escalus, upon the letter of the law, 'Your brother is a forfeit of the law'. (II.ii.71.) Against that law Isabella opposes one of the central doctrines of the religion she professes:

> Why, all the souls that were were forfeit once;
> And He that might the vantage best have took
> Found out the remedy. How would you be
> If He, which is the top of judgement, should
> But judge you as you are?   (II.ii. 73–7)

The doctrine of the atonement is that all souls, having transgressed God's law, would be subject to the damnation of his just judgement had not Christ interposed his own person and, by dying on the cross, atoned for all men, washing their sins away with his blood and permitting them to enter heaven. It seems impossible that an appeal so openly based upon one of the central tenets of Christianity could be rejected. It is, indeed, the first indication of the triumph of eternity which plays so large a part in the structure of the play.

Angelo remains unmoved because the argument is not immediately relevant. He has no designs upon Claudio's soul. He has already appointed him a confessor and provided 'needful but not lavish means' for the child that will eventually be born—which might mean that he regards the child as innocent and that therefore this precise Puritan does not believe in the doctrine of original sin. He is punishing the body for the sins of the body. The point is elaborated at some length in the case of Barnadine. They cannot execute him because, since he is drunk, he cannot be properly prepared by repentance and absolution for his passage to heaven. The Duke recognizes that 'to transport him in the mind he is were damnable.' (IV.iii.64.) It would condemn Barnadine to hell, but it would also damn those inhuman enough to kill his soul along with the body. It is a highly comic treatment of one of the central questions of the prayer scene in *Hamlet*.

Isabella's account of the way in which God has dealt measure for measure in his dealings with man is never directly answered. Instead Angelo offers in his turn another account of measure for measure; a classic account of the doctrine of deterrence and the way in which it ought to modify behaviour:

> The law hath not been dead, though it hath slept.
> Those many had not dar'd to do that evil
> If the first that did th'edict infringe
> Had answer'd for his deed. Now 'tis awake,
> Takes note of what is done, and, like a prophet
> Looks in a glass that shows what future evils—
> Either now or by remissness new conceiv'd,

And so in progress to be hatch'd and born—
Are now to have no successive degrees,
But ere they live, to end.   (II.ii.90–99)

To Isabella's image of Christ crucified Angelo opposes, without actually
answering her argument, a vision of the law as some kind of King Arthur
sleeping in the island valley of Avalon until waked by Merlin's prophecy
to foresee and overcome the danger that threatens in one last battle. This
image of doom is associated with the exercise of a repressive, excessive
and ineffectual law. The deterrence advocated by Angelo is, or can be, a
reasonable way of guiding human conduct. It has long been
demonstrated that mankind resembles other animals in adopting
behaviour which brings reward and avoiding that which has disagreeable
consequences. Even those who argue that the necessary control of
behaviour leads beyond human freedom and dignity emphasize that there
must be a close correlation between the form of behaviour and the
reward or punishment adopted. The law in Vienna proves an unsuitable
instrument for altering the powerfully conditioned behaviour of human
sexual response. Angelo parades the majestic force of a deterrent which
notably fails to deter Angelo.

It is this inflated air of false seeming which Isabella now instinctively
and correctly attacks:

                    Could great men thunder
        As Jove himself does, Jove would ne'er be quiet,
        For every pelting petty officer
        Would use his heaven for thunder,
        Nothing but thunder. Merciful Heaven,
        Thou rather, with thy sharp and sulphurous bolt,
        Splits the unwedgeable and gnarled oak
        Than the soft myrtle. But man, proud man,
        Dress'd in a little brief authority,
        Most ignorant of what he's most assur'd,
        His glassy essence, like an angry ape,
        Plays such fantastic tricks before high heaven
        As makes the angels weep; who, with our spleens,
        Would all themselves laugh mortal.   (II.ii.110–23)

It strikes exactly at the most vulnerable point of Angelo's argument and
turns his prophet looking in a glass into an inadequately clad ignoramus
making ape-like gestures. God created man in his own image, hence his

essence is a glass or mirror of the divine. Nothing is more certain about
man than this reflected perfection—and yet men remain obstinately
ignorant of the god-like behaviour appropriate for those in authority.
Man is traditionally supposed to be the ape, or imitator, of God. These
men, however, imitate the ritual gestures of aggression of the angry ape
and thus bring themselves below man, who was created a little lower
than the angels, since they are acting like beasts. Their beastliness is
exposed by the fact that the authority they are dressed in is so brief that it
reveals their genitals, as if Isabella were anticipating Angelo's coming
surrender to sexuality. In *Basilicon Doron* (p. 53) James argued that a
prince ought to teach by example since his people, like apes, would tend
to imitate his manners. Angelo is now about to imitate the behaviour of
the low and comic characters in a way which makes the angels weep but
which, had they the human spleen, would cause them literally to die of
laughing.

If Angelo exactly resembled the man described by Isabella then this
attack would destroy him as a dramatic character. The assault itself,
however, has started him upon the dangerous path of self knowledge:
'She speaks, and 'tis / Such sense that my sense breeds with it.'
(II.ii.140–41), an admission that Isabella's words have impregnated him
with sexual desire. The part of his character he now exposes is one which
he had striven all his life to repress and deny. Yet his fall from the pinnacle
of pride will turn out, however strangely, to be the first step on the way
to grace. The total ruin of this projected personality gives Angelo an odd
dramatic advantage over Isabella, whose virtue is still known to be
fugitive, cloistered and unbreathed. Isabella is totally unaware of the
sense in which she has just seduced Angelo. Shakespeare was well aware
of it—and expected his audience to recognize it. 'Hark how I'll bribe
you,' she says to Angelo, and means her bribe to be the power of prayer.
Angelo, Lucio and the audience all for an instant assume that she meant
something else. Angelo later corrects this view, arguing that Isabella is
clearly guiltless of any desire to tempt—but the temptation to which
Angelo now yields will shake Isabella to her soul. It will scour away the
proud preciseness which she shares with him. Only once they have both
learnt grace of Mariana will they have the power to unite the two
measures, of the law and of mercy, for which they have striven into that
union or harmony of the soul which does, or so the Florentine Platonists
believed, mirror the divine perfection.

Between this scene, in which Angelo is made pregnant with desire, and
his attempt to bring desire to its monstrous birth in the rape of Isabella,
is the scene in which the Duke attempts the religious task of reproaching

and relieving the distressed and pregnant Juliet. It opens with the
Provost's unequivocal praise of Claudio:

> a young man
> More fit to do another such offence
> Than die for this. (II.iii.13–15)

After this the comforts of religion, the insistence that Juliet should
recognize and repent of her sin, are bound to seem a little cold. The force
of the scene depends again upon the manipulation of incongruent
information. The audience knows that Juliet is married to Claudio.
Unaware of this *de praesenti* contract the Friar moralizes on repentance
and self pity but is sharply cut off:

> I do repent me as it is an evil,
> And take the shame with joy. (II.iii. 35–6)

Juliet's words must have the orthodox sense that she repents because it is
an evil—but 'as' also means 'if' and the sense that she 'only' requires to
repent 'in so far as' what she has done may be evil is strongly present in
the scene. The shame she takes with joy is the child she carries. Her few
but vital words give the audience a glimpse of love recognized and
mutual responsibility accepted. They create a powerful undercurrent of
hope which prepare for the moment when the love of Mariana turns the
tide of Angelo's lust.

In the sixth scene Angelo commented on the devil's cunning habit of
employing virtue to batter the defences of the virtuous. The eighth scene
reveals how he has profited from his new master's instruction. Isabella
offers to take on her own soul any sin incurred in sparing her brother.
Such vicarious afflictions are insufficient for Angelo's purpose and he
proposes that she should 'lay down the treasures of your body'
(II.iv.96). Isabella declares that she would choose martyrdom rather than
'yield my body up to shame'. There seems no reason to doubt her words.
She has given every indication of possessing the passion of martyrdom.
She cannot, however, choose it for herself. She must choose it for her
brother. It may be an awesome but admirable responsibility to wear the
marks of keen whips as rubies in a martyr's crown. It seems less saintly to
place that crown upon a head that must be removed from another's
shoulders. To die for a dearly held principle, or lay down a life for a
friend, is to obey forces stronger even than the primary law of self-
preservation. It may be right to lay down a friend's life for the health of
one's own soul, but it might also be called self-righteous. Chastity so
divine must appear slightly inhuman. When Isabella condemns her
brother for daring to beg his life on these terms it is evident that her

religious passion has driven out the charity which ought to accompany her faith and hope. Such is the power of Angelo's attack that Isabella can no longer keep time and measure in the harmony of God's grace.

It is a mark of Shakespeare's dramatic skill and supreme grasp of the psychological problem that he makes his heroine, at this stage of the play, weigh her chastity and charity in the balance and pronounce the measured yet discordant judgement, 'More than our brother is our chastity.' (II.iv.185.) The triumph of Isabella's chastity transforms Claudio's pageant into a triumph of death. She is a false Astraea because the hand that actually holds the balance of justice is not hers but Angelo's. This will be made clear with explosive force when the warrant for Claudio's execution arrives at the prison immediately after the supposed fall of her maidenhead. The effectiveness of that scene, however, depends upon the way it is prepared for here.

Angelo believes in her charity rather than her inhumanity. Mankind, he argues, is frail, and since he now believes that the broken reed of his own virtue represents the limits of human capacity he expects her to yield. In a remarkable speech she accepts the frailty of women:

> Ay, as the glassses where they view themselves,
> Which are as easy broke as they make forms.
> Women, help heaven! Men their creation mar
> In profiting by them. Nay, call us ten times frail;
> For we are soft as our complexions are,
> And credulous to false prints.   (II.iv.125–30)

Angelo accepts this as woman's submission to the triumph of love and urges her to show herself a woman by 'putting on the destin'd livery'. (II.iv.138.) He misunderstands Isabella's account of the reflexive power of women as much as he had failed to appreciate it in Mariana. Men mar their creation when they use their power to imprint or have reflected the image of their distorted wills and passions instead of the true copy of God's purpose. Angelo cannot use Isabella or Mariana in this way. They reflect the light of heaven which does, finally, find its reflection in Angelo's mind. Yet the power of ignorance is such that, without the intervention of the Duke, Angelo would have shattered both these frail glasses. Even as she resists his will Isabella cannot help reflecting his cruelty. She must now appear as the person whose sole judgement condemns Claudio to death.

With the end of this scene the measure of the law is complete and the measure of grace or mercy is about to begin. It turns upon one of the vital distinctions of the play:

> Ignominy in ransom and free pardon
> Are two houses: lawful mercy
> Is nothing kin to foul redemption.   (II.iv.111–13)

Isabella acts as Angelo's deputy in delivering judgement to Claudio, and even appears as his disciple in cruelty when she attacks her brother with words more bitter than any she could find against her judge. Yet her instinct is correct. The version of measure for measure proposed to her by Angelo is devilish and not merciful. It is not within her power to save her brother since the pardon he requires would not be bought by the ransom she is asked to pay. It is impossible to compromise with tyranny because no concession is ever sufficient to appease the tyrant's fear. It is fear which makes Angelo attempt to kill Claudio since he believes that such a triumph of death will allow him to live secure in the triumph of his good fame—a reputation for an icy virtue that cannot be touched by Isabella's accusation.

This bleak comfort of the certainty of death is not, however, available to Isabella when she has to answer the ill harmony of Angelo's proposal. That her decision, 'More than our brother is our chastity' is wrung from her with pain is shown by the fact that she carries it at once in all its terrible finality to her brother. If he accepts the necessity of his own death then she may feel justified in her resolve. There could be no clearer demonstration of a tyrant's power than the scene in prison where brother and sister ask of each other the impossible and are mutually disappointed. It is natural for Claudio to fear death as a fate worse than rape:

> Ay, but to die, and go we know not where;
> To lie in cold obstruction, and to rot;
> This sensible warm motion to become
> A kneaded clod; and the delighted spirit
> To bathe in fiery floods or to reside
> In thrilling region of thick ribbed ice;
> To be imprison'd in the viewless winds,
> And blown with restless violence round about
> The pendant world; or to be worse than worst
> Of those that lawless and incertain thought
> Imagine howling—'tis too horrible.
> The weariest and most loathed worldly life
> That age, ache, penury, and imprisonment,
> Can lay on nature is a paradise
> To what we fear of death.   (III.i.119–33)

He is appalled, as Hamlet was, by the dissolution of body and spirit and the possibility of the continuity of consciousness after death. Hamlet is disgusted by mankind's mortality. Claudio contemplates his own and the thought rightly terrifies him. His corruption and dissolution are the real price that has to be paid and he is given words to touch the audience with the consciousness of their own death. It is the coldest speech in Shakespeare. Only a heart of stone could resist it and it is inevitable that he should appeal for life to his sister and argue that:

> What sin you do to save a brother's life,
> Nature dispenses with the deed so far
> That it becomes a virtue.   (III.i.135–7)

This argument, that the saving of life is in itself merciful and gracious, had been used by Isabella to Angelo and then inverted, in more perverse fashion, by Angelo to Isabella. Hearing it now from Claudio she turns from him with a contemptuous violence of unchristian ferocity:

> Die; perish. Might but my bending down
> Reprieve thee from thy fate, it should proceed.   (III.i.145–6)

The words are unsympathetic, but they should not necessarily lose Isabella the sympathy of the audience. They are uncharacteristic and untrue. Isabella has already done a good deal of bending for her brother's life—to the extent of pleading in extenuation of the vice she most abhors. What Angelo and Claudio have demanded is that she commit that vice herself. This she cannot do, to save her brother or herself. Arguments about the sanctity or absurdity of chastity rather miss the point. As a matter of theology it seems probable that Angelo and Claudio are correct, to yield her virginity in these circumstances might be a sin, but hardly a damnable one. Claudio's appeal at least deserves sympathy, and its logic is hard to resist. Isabella's irrational outburst indicates that she is conditioned by a force strong enough to be compulsive. She understands the nature of Claudio's argument well enough. As A.D. Nuttall has pointed out, 'the poetry given to Isabel works as hard for Claudio as it does for her.' He argues that the lines:

> And the poor beetle that we tread upon
> In corporal sufferance finds a pang as great
> As when a giant dies.   (III.i.80–82)

must mean, in their historical context, that at death a giant feels no more pain than a beetle. Yet they also imply that a squashed beetle feels gigantic pain, and such is the fear of death that this seems the more natural way to read them.[22] There is nothing that can mediate between her passionate love for her brother, which she has amply demonstrated, and her compulsive chastity. Riven by these contradictory claims she turns in angry agony upon the person she most loves—as Hamlet turns upon Ophelia or Lear upon Cordelia. Like them, her rage is primarily directed against herself and the first thing that the Duke does when he steps forward to assume control of the action is to assure her that Angelo's offer was not genuine.

The Duke's role has obviously been carefully arranged for him by the dramatist. Having abandoned the law to Angelo he must himself now act as the instrument of grace which redeems the characters from the final penalty of judgement. In psychological terms, however, it is important that this is a role that he has found, or has been forced to assume, rather than one which he had planned from the beginning. This is the explanation of the absence of the normal comic forewarnings of his intentions in the opening scenes. It is also the source of the difficulty that critics have experienced with his character—the role of providence is played by a man evidently and consciously unworthy of it. This, of course, runs counter to his role as a Jamesian commentator; but the Duke is intended to be a ruler exercising the kingly gift who is worthy of the king's consideration. He is not a portrait of King James.

He began the play by appointing a deputy for himself in Vienna. He opens his new role by suggesting a deputy for Isabella in Angelo's bed. Both acts have caused scandal since the first appears weak and the second immoral. Neither of these firm judgements actually take account of the movement of measure for measure. On one level it can be maintained that the Duke has not abandoned his responsibility, only his apparent power, and he fulfils his obligation by providing Angelo with the opportunity of consummating his lawful marriage. On another level the scandalous imputation is accepted, incorporated into the action, and shown to be a part of the operation of grace which is perhaps beyond the comprehension of the 'unco guid'—who may, at this stage in the action, include Angelo and Isabella.

Denouncing her brother, Isabella is again responsible for one of the play's most significant phrases:

> Thy sin's not accidental, but a trade.
> Mercy to thee would prove itself a bawd.
> 'Tis best that thou diest quickly.   (III.i.150–53)

It does not seem accidental, but part of the dramatist's trade, that the

[22] 'Measure for Measure: Quid Pro Quo?', 248.

Duke should at this instant step forward and begin the process of acting as a bawd of mercy by proposing the substitution of Mariana. One of his reasons for doing so turns out to be the procuring of peace of mind and soul for Isabella. It has been maintained that she has just revealed a division in her nature between her chastity and her desire to save her brother, a split which has been evident since her first words of appeal to Angelo. Now a girl who is unable to reconcile her chastity with her desire is certainly not in a state of grace because one of the graces is missing. The philosophers, poets and artists of the Renaissance regularly used the figures of the three graces of classical myth as an image of the complex power of love. They are regularly shown, as in Botticelli's *Primavera*, as engaged in an eternal dance. In this dance the grace, *Castitas*, is opposed to *Voluptas* (passion, desire, will) but also joined to her through the mediating power of *Pulchritudo* or *Amor* (beauty or love). Within this dance, or measure, the contradictory aspects of the individual elements of love become complementary, harmonious and reconciled. For this concord to come out of discord all three are essential. Mariana is the classically Christian grace of love who keeps measure and proportion between the graces of chastity and passion so violently and fatally opposed in Angelo and Isabella.

Since the function of the grace of love is to procure the transformation of chastity into passion and yet keep them in harmony it might well be described as a bawd of mercy—the more so since passion, if left to itself, is liable to become the unrestrained figure of lust. In the situation faced by Isabella, mercy must prove itself a bawd of this kind before measure can answer to measure and the characters find grace. Mariana's part is essential since she converts the action of the play from a triumph of death to an eternal dance of the graces. It is evident, however, that she is not the only bawd of mercy in the play. Mistress Overdone and Pompey Bum are not simply the lowest strata in a comedy of hierarchical virtue. They, and their fellows, are an integral part of this pattern of grace. It is only necessary to compare Shakespeare with Cinthio, or examine Whetstone's use of his bawds and brothels, to realize that it is the structure of Renaissance philosophic images (the distinction of law and grace, the union of the tripartite life, the dance of the graces) which dramatically transmutes the old material of story into a play which fascinates and disturbs. It is these forces which subtly undermine the savage simplicity of the old style morality implicit in *Measure for Measure* and make it, as Erwin Panofsky has written of Titian's *Sacred and Profane Love*, 'not a document of neo-medieval moralism but of neo-Platonic humanism'.[23]

[23] Erwin Panofsky, *Problems in Titian: Mostly Iconographic* (New York 1969), p.119.

The most interesting, and the most significant, of these real bawds of
possible mercy is Lucio. His name, his conduct and his dramatic position
make him almost an allegorical figure in the play. Claudio's line, 'From
too much liberty, my Lucio, liberty', (I.ii.119) is in itself sufficient
evidence that the spirit of licence reigns in him—though it is an
instructive task to document it from the entire text. It is equally obvious
that he acts as a bawd of mercy when he carries Claudio's appeal for
assistance to Isabella. His opening words to her, 'Hail, virgin, if you be'
(I.iv.16), and his later excuse, 'I hold you as a thing enskied and sainted'
(I.iv.34) are an exact definition of his double role. It is, therefore, most
important that in the ninth scene he shows himself far from merciful to
Pompey, who appeals to him for bail as he is committed to prison by
Elbow. Lucio denies this suit on the grounds that 'it is not the wear'
(III.ii.69) since he accepts that Pompey is carried at the wheels of Caesar.
As a bawd, Pompey has become one of the captives in Angelo's presumed
triumph of chastity—and Lucio, determined to remain at liberty even
under the new order, willingly abandons his old companions. Whether
he wills it or not he has in this way become one of the instruments of the
new tyranny—irrespective of any consideration of Pompey's manifest
guilt under past, present or future attempts to impose a rule of law. It is a
brilliant condensed character portrait; whatever we may think of Lucio
when it is over it is clear that he is not as Pompey describes him, 'a
gentleman, and a friend of mine.' (III.ii.39.) Since tyranny is a kind of
license it finds it easy to conscript the licentious to its service.

Lucio now makes as important a contribution to the love debate as
Pompey's rout of Angelo and Escalus. In conversation with the Friar he
comments upon the absence of the Duke and the present severity. The
Friar argues that 'It is too general a vice, and severity must cure it'
(III.ii.93) to which Lucio replies, 'it is impossible to extirp it quite, friar,
till eating and drinking be put down.' (III.ii.95–7.) After retailing
reliable reports that Angelo is sterile and his urine congealed ice, he
breaks out:

> Why, what a ruthless thing is this in him, for the rebellion of a
> codpiece to take away the life of a man? Would the Duke that is
> absent have done this?   (III.ii.106–8)

Lucio then develops the interesting argument that the Duke would not
have done it because he was himself a lecher, a drunkard and 'a very
superficial, ignorant, unweighing fellow.' (III.ii.130.)

Now it is evident that these accusations are not true, any more than
Lucio's certain knowledge of Angelo's urine is correct. Yet the Duke's

leap to his own defence, 'Let him be but testimonied in his own bringings-forth, and he shall appear to the envious a scholar, a statesman, and a soldier' (III.ii.134–6), fails to carry total conviction. It is, after all, the Duke's failure to act as the complete master of the tripartite life that accounts for his presence in the disguise of a friar while Angelo governs the dukedom. At this point Lucio's victory is more complete than Pompey's since there is no dramatic possibility of the Duke appearing as the triumphant conqueror. It is true that, as Lucio consigned Pompey to the wheels of Caesar, so he will be made captive in his own turn. Yet his words strike a blow for truth and freedom although he also buckles to their service a slanderous invention which, if allowed its permissive pass, would obliterate both. He has, moreover, as he confesses to the Friar, had a child by the whore Kate Keepdown. According to Mistress Overdone, who brought up the infant (thus proving herself a bawd of mercy), he also promised Kate marriage. Lucio is thus the exact counterpart of Claudio—he has committed the fornication for which Claudio is condemned. Yet it is also part of his role to pull the hood off the Friar and discover the Duke. In his role of freedom, liberty and license he touches the highest and lowest points of the play's moral scale. He is the free friend who brings Isabella to redeem her brother and he is the Friar's false companion whose envious vision of the world is as distorted as Iago's. Free (as his name suggests) he is both truth and slander the Blatant Beast of Book Five of Spenser's *Fairie Queene* whose crime of false report was both feared and ruthlessly punished by King James. He stands exactly at the play's point of balance, between truth and falsehood, between the court and the stews, and acts both as a bawd of mercy and, like a kind of burr, as the merciless pandar of lies.

This double role played by the bawds is emphasized by the fate of Pompey. Finally convicted, he is turned from pimp to deputy assistant executioner. Confronted by his new apprentice the professional Abhorson passes one of the most measured and significant judgements in the play: 'A bawd, sir? Fie upon him! He will discredit our mystery.' (IV.i.25.) Pompey objects, since he claims to have followed a profession which is also a mystery since it is to imitate the union of beauty and passion that whores paint their faces. He is, however, perfectly willing to learn this new trade in which the mystery of justice is apparently served by the removal of the whole head. In his role as bawd Pompey had been responsible for the notable defeat of Angelo and Escalus on the bench of justice. As the law's new instrument he is himself conquered by the drunken, blasphemous, and murderous Barnadine. 'A man that apprehends death no more dreadfully but as a drunken sleep'

(IV.ii.135–6) is evidently part of the unacceptable dregs of society. Yet the authorities cannot execute him since, by transporting his unprepared soul to hell, they would inevitably condemn themselves to eternal damnation. It is another crushing victory for the forces of anarchy, and at the same time a revelation of the all conquering mystery of grace. The law and axe prove unsuitable instruments for controlling the rebellion of a codpiece or terminating a drunken oblivion. Good government must find some measure through which even these discordant elements can be harmonized in the conjunction of chastity, charity and the passionate consummation of love.

By their conduct these characters define in comic terms the serious extremes which are touched by Mariana in her role as bawd of mercy. She plays the part of a whore to unite Angelo through the freedom of her body in the perfect service of marriage. Introduced in the tenth scene of the play by a song which treats of love rejected and despised she demonstrates her flawless constancy by the willing substitution of her body for Isabella's in that secret summer house bed. The bed-trick, as it has been called, is not a simple piece of conjuring but a process of spiritual alchemy. In the performance of two swift physical acts Angelo appears to have transformed himself into a rapist and murderer. He finds that he has been transmuted into a husband and a criminal reprieved, like Barnadine, under the very edge of the axe.

It is natural that Mariana should ask for mercy for her husband. Her remarkable phrase, 'I crave no other, nor no better man' (V.i.424), acknowledges for the audience the strength so evidently present in the character of Angelo. It is equally inevitable that the Duke should reject this plea couched in the exact terms of Isabella's original plea for Claudio, concentrating upon the character of the criminal rather than his crime. The words of the returned prince assert the triumph of law:

> The very mercy of the law cries out
> Most audible, even from his proper tongue,
> 'An Angelo for Claudio, death for death!'
> Haste still pays haste, and leisure answers leisure;
> Like doth quit like, and Measure still for Measure. (V.i.405–9)

This is the only occasion in the play where the words, measure for measure, are used and it is surely significant that they are placed in a context where they cannot be true. The audience knows that Claudio is alive and that while the Duke's words follow the pattern of the Old Testament doctrine of Leviticus 24. 19–20, 'eye for eye, tooth for tooth' his intentions are those of the New Testament, Matthew 7,1-1:

Judge not, that ye be not judged. For with what judgement ye judge, ye shall be judged: and with what measure ye mete, it shall be measured to you again.

Like *The Merchant of Venice* or *The Tempest, Measure for Measure* is a revenge comedy which dramatizes, in literal terms, the repetitive futility of a justice which depends upon the exchange of dead men's heads. This deliberate false concord rests the weight of moral decision in the play, for the second time, upon Isabella.

Believing her brother to be dead, she now kneels to save Mariana's marriage precisely as Mariana had preserved Isabella's chastity. In accordance with her nature as the chaste virgin, Astraea, Isabella's appeal to the Duke is not for mercy, but justice. The two kneeling girls thus form an expressive emblem of the interdependence of mercy and justice. It is essential that the audience should see Isabella still capable of functioning in a world where Claudio is dead. His resurrection should then be the mediating power which accomplished the final transformation of Isabella into the chaste, beautiful and passionate figure who accepts the hand of the Duke in marriage. The hidden Claudio can now openly celebrate his marriage to his pregnant Juliet. Mercy and transgression are already united in Angelo and Mariana, liberty and licence are included and controlled within that formal bond by the marriage of Lucio and Kate Keepdown. Eight individuals, the number of justice, form four couples, the number of concord and as power and justice are finally united by love in the persons of the Duke and Isabella, measure for measure is formally completed.

The Duke has often been blamed for brutal insensitivity when he fails to inform Isabella of Claudio's escape. It is possible that the structure of incongruent information does creak a little but it should be observed that he is not simply testing Isabella, which could be called sadistic, but transforming her. For all of the characters the way of grace lies through the shadow of death. It is a severe and painful process which none can escape. As in the tragedies, human virtue is tempered in the cold reality of death until it is bright and strong enough to form part of the triumph of eternity. The Duke himself does not escape this tempering process. His whole progress of abdication and triumphal return unites the active, contemplative and passionate sides of his nature so that he is capable of stretching out his hand to Isabella. The dribbling dart of love has pierced and made complete his heart. The emblematic soliloquy, 'He who the sword of heaven would bear' at the end of the ninth scene is not a smug piece of self-congratulation but an awareness of the weight of the burden that he must now carry. In the stews of Vienna he receives a necessary education in human functions which are normally hidden under the art of 'seeming' and becomes a true head of state capable of reforming the elbow, restraining the liberty of the codpiece, and moderating the stink of the bum in the body politic.

Yet, though the formal pattern of the play requires Isabella to take the Duke's hand, it is surprising and significant that there is no speech of acceptance or surrender by the heroine to the man she loves. In this respect *Measure for Measure* is unique among Shakespeare's comedies. This has led some directors to stage an ending in which Isabella appears to reject the Duke. This possibility is also, I believe, a deliberate part of Shakespeare's pattern. In 1604 it was common to compliment King James by asserting that he had united justice and mercy. *Measure for Measure* points out that the task of government is to achieve such a union, and demands of any potential ruler in the audience whether he thinks he is capable of creating it. As it turned out, it proved to be a task beyond the power of the Stuart kings.

The Duke must appear 'like power divine' not because he is God, but because he is God's deputy who has the same task to perform in the state as the Renaissance neo-Platonists believed God performed in his creation—the 'tuning of the world' as Robert Fludd calls it in *Utriusque Cosmi Historia*. The kind of tuning envisaged by Shakespeare may perhaps be illustrated by Richard Hooker's discussion, in the first book of his *Ecclesiastical Polity*, of the nature of Christ's commandment to love our neighbours as ourselves:

> If I do harm, I must look to suffer; there being no reason that others should show greater measure of love to me, than they have by me showed unto them. My desire, therefore, to be loved of my equals in nature as much as possible may be, imposeth upon me a natural duty of bearing to them-ward fully the like affection.

It is a transaction in which short measure is too often given and received. The abdication and return of the Duke is a triumphal form giving expression to the serious necessity and comic impossibility of such a task. Out of this concordant discord in human nature Shakespeare created the dramatic harmony of *Measure for Measure*.

Bibliography

Editions

R. C. Bald (Pelican) New York 1956.

Ernst Leisi, *'Measure for Measure': An Old-Spelling and Old Meaning Edition*, Heidelberg 1964.

J. W. Lever (Arden) 1965.

J. M. Nosworthy (New Penguin) London 1969.

Critical and other works

Albrecht, L., *Neue Untersuchungen zu Shakespeares Mass für Mass*, Berlin 1914.

Alexander, Peter, 'Measure for Measure: A case for the Scottish Solomon', *Modern Language Quarterly* 28 (1967) 478–88.

Bennett, Josephine Waters, *'Measure for Measure' as Royal Entertainment*, New York 1966.

Carnicelli, D. D., *Lord Morley's 'Tryumphes of Fraunces [Petrarcke'*, Cambridge, Mass. 1971.

Chambers, R. W., 'The Jacobean Shakespeare and *Measure for Measure*' (British Academy Lecture) London 1937.

Craigie, J., *The Basilicon Doron of King James VI* (Scottish Text Society), Edinburgh 1944.

Evans, Bertrand, *Shakespeare's Comedies*, Oxford 1960.

Fowler, Alastair, *Triumphal Forms*, Cambridge 1970.

Gordon, D. J., 'The Imagery of Ben Jonson's *The Masque of Blacknesse* and *The Masque of Beautie*', *Journal of the Warburg and Courtauld Institutes* 6 (1943), 122–41.

Jones, Emrys, *Scenic Form in Shakespeare*, Oxford 1971.

Lascelles, Mary, *Shakespeare's 'Measure for Measure'*, London 1953.

Lawrence, W. W., *Shakespeare's Problem Comedies*, London 1931.

Levin, Richard, 'The King James Version of *Measure for Measure*', *Clio* 3 (1974), 134–66.

Macrobius, *Commentary on the Dream of Scipio*, tr. and ed. W. H. Stahl, New York 1952.

Miles, Rosalind, *The Criticism of 'Measure for Measure'*, M.A. Thesis (University of Birmingham) 1966.

Miles, Rosalind, *A Study of 'Measure for Measure'*, Ph.D. Thesis (University of Birmingham) 1968.

Nichols, John, *The Progresses, Processions, and Magnificent Festivities of King James the First*, London 1828.

Noble, Richmond, *Shakespeare's Biblical Knowledge*, New York 1935.

Nuttall, A. D., '*Measure for Measure*: Quid pro Quo?' *Shakespeare Studies* 4, ed. J. Leeds Barroll, Cincinnati, Ohio 1968, 231–51.

Panofsky, Erwin, *Problems in Titian: Mostly Iconographic*, New York 1969.

Ringler, W. A., *The Poems of Sir Philip Sidney*, Oxford 1960.

Rose, M., *Shakespearean Design*, Cambridge, Mass. 1972.

Schanzer, Ernest, 'The Marriage-Contracts in *Measure for Measure*', *Shakespeare Survey 13*, ed. Allardyce Nicoll, Cambridge 1960, 81–9.

Stevenson, D. L., *The Achievement of Shakespeare's 'Measure for Measure'*, Ithaca, N. Y. 1966.

Weil, Herbert S., Jr, 'The Options of the Audience: Theory and Practice in Peter Brook's *Measure for Measure*', *Shakespeare Survey 25*, ed. Kenneth Muir, Cambridge 1972, 27–35.

Wickham, Glynne, *Early English Stages* (3 vols), London 1959– .

Yates, Frances A., *Astraea: The Imperial Theme in the Sixteenth Century*, London 1975.

Index